This book is dedicated to the members of the Connor House *Class of '62*,
who shared my journey through the Sixties and beyond,
and also to our late headmaster Mr Gordon Thomson (1915-2009)
- my mentor and friend.

Contents

Introduction

IN time-honoured tradition Terence Bowman, younger and smarter brother of contributor Geoffrey Bowman, exercised the right of the second son to be different.

After contributing a number of stories to the *County Down Spectator*, he chose not to follow the career path taken by his late father Hugh, a top barrister and QC by his mid-40s, opting instead for journalism. He joined the *Mourne Observer* in Newcastle in 1976 – his first and only job – rising in the 1980s to the position of Editor.

His first venture into the world of books was "Railway Memories" (1991), a compilation of features from the *Mourne Observer*, which he edited, followed in 1997 by "People's Champion" (Ulster Historical Foundation), his own biography of his great grandfather, Alexander Bowman, a pioneer of labour politics in Ireland. Further local publications have followed, but "Bangor in the Sixties" reflects the fact that he has never forgotten the town where he was born and reared.

ON a blustery Friday morning in February 1968, a month before my eleventh birthday, one of the teachers at Connor House handed me a ten shilling note and sent me out of school to do a message. There was no question of a signed letter being required from the headmaster or parental approval being sought before I ventured out alone onto Clifton Road.

As a trusted P7 pupil, in my final months before moving on to the 'big school', this was a normal way of spending my break time. Even the teacher's shopping list, a *News Letter*, a *Co Down Spectator*, 20 Kensitas and 20 Silk Cut – "and you can keep the change" – was very much par for the Sixties course.

Socks pulled up and cap fastened tightly to my head, I followed the well-trodden path down to Wray Parke's shop on High Street, crossing several roads and intersections along the way and exchanging greetings with a few other short-trousered pupils on similar missions.

It was a case of like father, like son, for it was the same shop my Dad visited each weekday evening on his way home from work, buying similar items to those I'd been tasked to buy that morning, except the gold-boxed Benson and Hedges was his preferred

Wray Parke's at High Street – one of a series of shop fronts, photographed for Bangor Borough Council in 1962, that feature in "Bangor in the Sixties." They appear courtesy of the North Down Museum.

brand of cigarette and the *Belfast Telegraph* took the place of the *News Letter*.

Fast forward more than 40 years and, judged by today's standards, the criminal offences committed during my 15 minutes of freedom beyond the school gates begin to mount up. The teacher and the headmaster, by association, for allowing me to leave school unaccompanied and without my parents' knowledge; the school and the education authority for permitting the teacher to act in such a reckless fashion; the shop for serving cigarettes to a minor... not to mention the teacher's likely intention to smoke the cigarettes in the staff room while reading the papers.

Having spent the best part of a year reliving the Sixties while writing and compiling this book, I can think of no simpler example of how our lives and customs have changed in the intervening decades. And with the 50th anniversary of that momentous period now upon us, there is no better time to reflect on what the Sixties meant to those of us who lived through such special years in Bangor. For many, including myself, it represented the time of our lives; to the remainder there is no denying the Sixties were completely different to any other decade, before or after.

None of this would have been possible without the support of the North Down Museum, which made available to me the complete files for every copy of the *Spectator* published between January 1960 and December 1969. Grateful thanks go to the newspaper itself and to its former reporters who have contributed their Sixties memories to the book; likewise to the Local Studies staff at Library Headquarters in Ballynahinch for their valuable assistance.

My thanks also go to the numerous other contributors – men and women from all walks of life – who share their thoughts on the Bangor they knew in the 1960s. Some still live in the town, while others have settled elsewhere. To all it was clearly a special period in their lives.

I'd like to give a special mention to Jonathan Coates, of the *Newtownards Chronicle,* who sought out many of the pictures from the *Spectator* archive, and my former colleague Niki Hill, who read over the copy and proved the point that even editors need to be edited!

I should add that, with the passage of time, the mind has a habit of playing tricks on you. I learned during my journey through the Sixties that some things simply did not happen as I remembered them. Items gleaned from the pages of the *Spectator* are retold as they were reported; personal memory lapses are an entirely different, and forgivable, matter!

Terence Bowman today.

Terence and Geoffrey Bowman pictured in Donegal in 1963 – debate rages over which brother is the smarter of the two.

Foreword

By Ian Wilson, Manager, North Down Museum (and a Bangor teenager in the Sixties)

IAN Wilson attended Ballyholme Primary School, Bangor Grammar School and Queen's University. After teaching English and History at Coleraine Inst. for nine years, he returned to Bangor to take charge of the Council's new Heritage Centre (renamed in 2007 the North Down Museum).

His main personal research interest is Irish maritime studies, and he is the author of 'Shipwrecks of the Ulster Coast' and 'Donegal Shipwrecks', and co-author of 'Ships and Quaysides of Ulster.' He also writes short stories (and occasionally they have been published!). He suspects life's excitement levels may have peaked at the age of 13 when seeing The Beatles at the King's Hall in the '60s, at the height of Beatlemania! See picture on page 14.

THE winter of 1962-63 was the coldest since 1740. From Boxing Day till early March, Siberian winds bore in regular heavy snowfalls. The British Isles shivered.

On Wednesday 6 February 1963, Bangor was isolated apart from the railway; all movement by road was impossible. The sea froze in Sandeel Bay, between Groomsport and Orlock. Milkmen pulled their crates on sleighs, or sold direct to snowy figures struggling through the streets.

Meanwhile, at Bangor Grammar School, formidable headmaster Randall Clarke commanded the gates be opened as usual. It was on this day of all days that the satirical, irreverent new world of the Sixties, later and forever dubbed 'The Swinging Sixties,' first tried to infiltrate Mr Clarke's austere domain…

There is a tempting case for suggesting that the Sixties only began in earnest with the great thaw in the early Spring of 1963. On 11 January, The Beatles had released their first big hit, 'Please Please Me,' and a week later made their first major television appearance on *Thank Your Lucky Stars.*

In early February, navigating icy roads, they began their first British tour, with Helen Shapiro topping the bill. On 22 March, Secretary of State for War John Profumo lied to the House of Commons when he announced there was 'no impropriety whatsoever' in his relationship with Christine Keeler.

Latest SPRING Models
SHOES
ARRIVING DAILY
WARNER'S
MAIN STREET · BANGOR

THE COUNTY DOWN SPECTATOR AND ULSTER STANDARD

BLAXNIT Long Life SOCKS

PRICE: FOURPENCE

"THE SPECTATOR," FRIDAY, 8th FEBRUARY, 1963

B-r-r... FREEZE SIEGE ISOLATES BANGOR

Railway only outside link

ALL ROADS OUT OF THE TOWN IMPASSABLE ... ELECTRICITY BLACK-OUTS ... TELEPHONE SERVICES CUT ... SHORTAGES OF BREAD AND MILK. THESE WERE JUST A FEW OF THE INCONVENIENCES SUFFERED AS BANGOR WAS VIRTUALLY ISOLATED BY SNOW DRIFTS AFTER TUESDAY'S BLIZZARD, DESCRIBED BY MANY OLD RESIDENTS AS "THE WORST IN LIVING MEMORY."

POLICE ANSWER EMERGENCY CALLS

Controlling the thaw

What a night it was!

Fatality at railway station

MEETINGS CANCELLED

FIREMEN STAND-BY

Military and police help in Holywood

OPEN AGAIN

Controversial decision delayed to test public opinion

OPEN ON A SUNDAY PROPOSAL FOR BANGOR SPORTS

PEGGY PAGE

Anne Roulston

WARNER'S
Announce the arrival this week of the new Spring Models
CLARKS
NORVIC
KREVITT
LOTUS
GOLD CROSS
VAN DAL
MAIN STREET :: BANGOR

The Profumo Affair, the scandal against which all others since have been measured, was seized on by the new magazine *Private Eye* and *That Was the Week That Was*, the late-night satirical television programme, which was first broadcast in November 1962. It achieved phenomenal popularity with around 12 million viewers tuning in to see a 23-year-old David Frost (as sudden a national celebrity as The Beatles) and his colleagues poke fun at Britain's Establishment.

Blowing in the wind, there was a feeling that anything was possible; nothing was safe. Not even the teaching staff at Bangor Grammar School were safe!

My efforts to venture in that Arctic Wednesday – perhaps a little reluctant – were in vain. Later, a First Form colleague phoned me. Even before we discussed the Top Twenty (I find 'Diamonds' by former Shadows Jet Harris and Tony Meehan was Number One), he was just bursting with excitement at what had happened in school, to which he had successfully trekked, along with a small number of other gallant 'swots.'

"Wait till you hear this! Some Sixth Formers were selling a wee magazine they printed, about the teachers. It's called 'That Was', you know like the David Frost programme. It makes fun of old George, and 'Yogi' Hawthorne, and Miss Tipping and all... I bought one for three d. 'Woody' Woodburn lent me the money!"

Next day, Thursday 7 February 1963, the elements

had relented. I made it in. All the chatter was about *That Was* as it passed around inky schoolboy hands. The staff had indeed been lampooned and debunked, *Private Eye*-style, by the budding satirists of the Upper Sixth.

One story stood out. It concerned our English teacher, Mr George Heuston, a man keen on field sports who, allegedly, had shot his own gundog.

Just after lunch our class lined up outside Mr Heuston's classroom, waiting for him to unlock the door. Standing with us was a very tall, thin Sixth Former holding an envelope. As Mr Heuston approached in his solemn way, gowned and clutching chalk-dusted exercise books, the youth stepped forward.

"Mr Heuston, I'd like to give you this apology!"

George Heuston regarded him sorrowfully.

"It really doesn't matter", he quietly stated, *"I've already taken legal advice."*

The satirist departed, crushed. Twenty-eight First Formers stood in shocked silence.

That evening I related the startling events to my father.

".... I've already taken legal advice."

To my surprise, my father roared with laughter!

"What did he say again?"

"I've already taken legal advice," I repeated in that soft yet doom-laden manner. My father laughed even more heartily! He knew George Heuston, and spotted at once this was but a massive bluff. For ages afterwards, my father, when in need of a laugh, asked me to repeat the scene.

The first issue was also the last issue of *That Was.* The satire revolution of the Sixties had even tried, in Bob Dylan's words, to shake the windows and rattle the walls of Bangor Grammar School (Bob Dylan was in England for the first time that freezing winter, and helped demolish an old piano for firewood in an unheated flat).

That the times were indeed a-changing is a theme of

Ian Wilson in his student days.

Mr George Heuston. Picture courtesy of Bangor Grammar School archives.

Fans of The Beatles at their King's Hall concert in 1964. Ian Wilson was among them.
Spectator picture

Terence Bowman's splendid, evocative book. The North Down Museum has been pleased to facilitate his journey through all the back numbers of the *Co Down Spectator* from the Sixties and to seek out photographs.

No researcher could have been more diligent and enthusiastic about his subject. This certainly comes across, not only in the narrative, but also his inspired idea to feature specific memories of well-known local people who grew up in the decade. As Wordsworth wrote of an earlier era (and here George Heuston would be proud of the First Former left speechless outside his classroom):

'Bliss was it in that dawn to be alive
But to be young was very heaven.'

That will not be everyone's experience of the Sixties, but I do think the decade, especially the years 1963-1967, was a period of enormous vitality, optimism and progress in so many spheres – and a wonderful time to be growing up.

1960

...the Spectator reports

Terry Neill, aged 19, coaches local youngsters at Ballyholme Park during a home visit shortly after signing for Arsenal. *Spectator* picture

BANGOR-BORN Terry Neill, from Hazelbrook Avenue, was still in the headlines in January, having been transferred from Bangor FC to Arsenal the previous month for a fee of £2,500. His earliest football had been with 1st Bangor Boys' Brigade and then Bangor FC during the 1958/59 and 1959/60 seasons. Neill made his First Division debut against Sheffield Wednesday on 23 December 1960, aged 18.

Market Day in Bangor in the early 1960s. The houses in the background were set to be demolished to be replaced by shops and maisonettes. *Spectator* picture.

Bangor Borough Council gave its approval in January for a redevelopment programme costing £250,000 for the Castle Street/ Castle Square area. The proposals envisaged the creation of a pedestrian precinct from Market Street to Castle Street, along with a covered market hall and an adjacent fire station (to be built by the Northern Ireland Fire Authority for £258,000).

By advertising for senior and junior engineers in early February, Bangor Borough Council signalled its intention to commence a 10-year project to build a ring road to link the Belfast Road with the Groomsport Road, via the Clandeboye, Newtownards, Bloomfield, Gransha and Donaghadee Roads. Seven months later the Ministry of Commerce agreed in principle with the Council's proposals; completion was expected by the end of the Sixties.

Saturday 2 April marked the closure of the Adelphi Cinema on lower Main Street. The Tudor Cinema, also on lower Main Street, would screen its final films on Saturday 15 September 1962, leaving Bangor with just two cinemas, the Tonic on Hamilton Road, and the Queen's on Queen's Parade.

Seventeen-year-old Patricia Mencarelli, daughter of Mr and Mrs Amadeo (Andy) Mencarelli, of Bridge Street, modelled the latest fashions on a new Ulster Television series called *A Matter of Taste,* which began on Monday 4 April. The former Glenlola Collegiate student was preparing to leave for Florence that September to study music and art.

The removal of the wall separating Abbey Street from Castle Park, for a street widening scheme, required the felling of several trees in April, but the work revealed a magnificent view of the park.

Manse Hill at Ballygilbert was levelled in May as part of the construction contract for the new dual carriageway to Bangor. The work also necessitated the demolition of the century-old Clandeboye Post Office.

AND ULSTER STANDARD

"THE SPECTATOR," FRIDAY, 5th AUGUST, 1960

"Who's up there?" enquired Earl Mountbatten, when his attention was drawn to a photographer on the balcony of Mountbatten House. The occasion was Earl Mountbatten's visit, last Friday, to the Royal Naval Association's Bangor Headquarters named after him.

"Spectator" Photo.

Earl Mountbatten's flying visit to Bangor

Earl Mountbatten visited Bangor on 29 June, landing by helicopter at the Luke's Point car park. He inspected the redecorated headquarters of the Royal Naval Association's Bangor branch at Queen's Parade, named Mountbatten House in his honour. He was welcomed by Mayor Charles Valentine and 'piped aboard' the new HQ by Shipmate James Norman.

A busy Queen's Parade in the summer of 1960.
Spectator picture.

Rathgael House, a large old mansion on the outskirts of Bangor, was demolished in August to make way for a new training school for "Protestant non-Borstal boys." The 36-acre site on the Rathgael Road was acquired by the board of management of the Malone Training School in Belfast, which it was replacing.

Former Bangor Drama Club member Colin Bleakley, who had just turned 30, appeared in "Lena, O My Lena," the *Armchair Theatre* play on Channel Nine (ITV) on Sunday 25 September. It was just his fourth appearance on television and it was followed that October with a part in Eugene O'Neill's 'Moon for the Misbegotten' on the BBC. There would be many more television and film roles during the Sixties.

Work was completed on the new Special Care Centre at the High Street end of the Ballyholme Road. The previous centre had operated for five years in the former Astor Cinema premises on the Seacliff Road, catering for children from Bangor, Dundonald, Holywood, Newtownards, Comber, Donaghadee and district.

Pupils of Trinity Primary School ready for the new school year in September 1961.
Spectator picture.

One of Bangor's oldest and most familiar corners, at the junction of Church Street and the Newtownards Road, was given a facelift in October with the demolition of two houses to provide a better view for motorists. In addition, a stream at the rear of Bertie Campbell's pharmacy business on the Belfast Road was piped in and parking space was provided for 10 cars.

The new £158,000 St Columbanus Secondary Intermediate School, catering for 360 boys and girls from the Catholic parishes of Bangor, Newtownards and Holywood, was blessed and formally opened on Tuesday 29 November by Most Rev. Dr Daniel Mageean, Bishop of Down and Connor. It occupied a 13.5 acre site on the Ballymaconnell Road.

Local children enjoy the first heavy snowfall of winter 1960/61 at Castle Park, Bangor. On the left, Elliott Reynolds pushes Trevor Gray and Alan McConnell, while, on the right, Gordon Andrews does the same for brother and sister Michael and Deirdre Lindsay. Included is dog Susie.
Spectator picture.

Alan Gadsby
...remembers

AFTER leaving the RAF in the mid-1970s, Alan Gadsby went into the hotel business, winning an Innkeeper of the Year award for his "lovely wee country inn" at Dunster near Minehead in Somerset.

He emigrated to Australia in 1980 where his first job in Adelaide was as manager of a crematorium. He got into comedy at a time when Irish comedian Hal Roach was all the rage. He progressed into musical comedy and, being Irish, had great success. Now he is known far and wide as Irish Albert and even his own granddaughter calls him Grandpa Albert. He has performed on cruise ships and on television. Alan's website is www.irishalbert.com.

ALTHOUGH I've lived in Australia for some 30 years, I still have fond memories of my childhood days in Bangor during the early Sixties, although they didn't last too long as I'd joined the RAF by 1962, when I was still only 15.

Many people knew me by the nickname 'The Mouse' when I attended Central Primary School, Ballyholme Primary School and Bangor Tech. I was always a keen footballer and was in the team which made history by winning the Knockout Cup that involved all the big Belfast schools. It had never been done before. One of my team mates was Billy McCamley who later played for Bangor and Scunthorpe.

By the end of 1960 I was working on the dodgems in Barry's and at the pongo [bingo] in the Palladium. The following year I got barred with a friend from the Tonic for unscrewing the numbers from the

Lyn Glithero in the early 1960s and now. Right: Alan Gadsby after joining the RAF.

backs of all the seats. It was my dad who told on me!

I was in First Bangor BB and played drums in the band. My nickname by then was Little Woo and I fell in love with a beautiful girl called Lyn Glithero, who had long blonde hair and a smile you could never forget!

On Sundays all the boys would sit on the wall at Queen's Parade, from the bottom of Main Street round to Pickie Pool. The girls would walk along with their friends strutting their stuff while we were eating our four-penny bags of chips from Greezy Joe's or an ice cream from Wests'.

Both were opposite the big clock. However, the best fish and chip shop was the Magnet, which was up the lane beside Greezy Joe's and opposite a bookies. We used to go into Greezy Joe's store room and nick all the empty lemonade bottles, then take them back to his shop and get the penny refunds!

The other good pick-up place was at the square dancing outside Pickie Pool. They were great times indeed!

I also remember Cecil Greenwood's wee shop on High Street, where we could swap our comic books. He used to paint the front of his head black to match his receding hair line.

The big influence on my later career in

Young people on the wall at Queen's Parade – a popular Sixties meeting place.
Picture courtesy of Colin Barnes.

Alan Gadsby as entertainer Irish Albert portraying the Queen.

entertainment would have been James Young, who brought his shows to Bangor in the late 1950s and early 1960s.

I joined the RAF at the age 15 as a would-be electronics engineer. The only reason for this was that the officer in charge said: "Right, you lot over here will be cooks, you lot over there will be aircraft fitters and you other lot will be in electronics. I got into the RAF soccer team and won the RAF boxing lightweight title. I spent four years in Scotland in the RAF and just played sport. I knew nothing about electronics!

1961

...the Spectator reports

Members of Trinity Presbyterian Church, at their annual meeting on 22 February, learned of plans for a new hall on the site of the adjoining Adelphi Cinema premises. The cinema building, which cost the church £1,415 plus £38 a year in ground rent, was deemed unsuitable for conversion and was demolished.

Donna Douglas, 18-year-old daughter of Mr and Mrs Jim Douglas, of Rugby Avenue, travelled to England in March to appear on a South Eastern Television programme with bandleader Max Jaffa. The talented teenager, who had begun her singing career with the Abbey Youth Choir, had already appeared on UTV's *Crossroads*, singing "Paper Roses" and "Nora Malone." That September Donna sang her latest

Donna Douglas (right) during a visit in May 1963 to the record department of F. C. McCutcheon and Co., Main Street. Included is assistant Mrs Mary Collins.
Spectator picture.

record, "Tammy Tell Me True," on Independent Television's *Thank Your Lucky Stars* and it was also played on the BBC's *Juke Box Jury*. It was her fourth record and by the end of the year she had also appeared on the BBC's *The Six-Five Special*.

At the beginning of May Bangor Borough Council decided to defer a proposal to fluoridate the local water supply. A number of Councils had already voted against fluoridation, although Cllr Andy Templeton contended that opponents were "a very tiny but noisy minority." No decision was ever taken to add fluoride to local water.

Twins Maurice and Anthony Butler (18), of Hamilton Villas, Groomsport Road, took part in ITV's *Double Your Money* in May. After answering six general knowledge questions correctly, they won £32.

Bangor nonagenarian John Agnew.
Spectator picture.

Widely reckoned in May to be the town's oldest man, Mr John Agnew, of 72 Abbey Street, could remember a time when Bangor had one grocery shop, Hugh Furey's, and the cost of a return train ticket to Belfast was 8d. Born in 1863 at King Street, when it was known as West Street, he had lived in Bangor all his life. Mr Agnew died on 14 September 1962, a month short of his one hundredth birthday.

Last day at the PNEU school in 1961.

The PNEU (Parents' National Education Union) School at Farnham Park closed in June. The school had opened in October 1940, with some 240 children in total, from as far as Ballyholme and Crawfordsburn, receiving sole instruction from Miss Maureen Fetherstonhaugh. She became teacher for the new P2 (kindergarten) class at Connor House.

Bertram Mills' world famous circus, starring the legendary Coco the Clown, visited Ireland for the first time, with three days being spent in Bangor (17-19 July). In a reflection of the time, the circus featured elephants, chimpanzees, horses and other animals, as well as human performers. Coco visited Pickie Pool, arriving in a carriage pulled by four miniature ponies, and spoke to a large group of children about road safety.

The Queen and Prince Philip leave Bangor Harbour for lunch on the Royal Yacht *Britannia*.
Spectator picture.

The Queen and Prince Philip travelled to Bangor on 9 August – it was the first royal visit to the town since 1903, when King Edward VII drove through the main streets to the North Pier for embarkation on the Royal Yacht.

Having arrived by car at Bangor Castle to meet Mayor Charles Valentine and members of the Borough Council, the couple travelled down Main Street and along Bridge Street, past cheering crowds, to Quay Street where they boarded a launch at the Central Pier, which took them out to *Britannia* for lunch.

They later travelled by the somewhat circuitous route of Quay Street, High Street and Clifton Road to the Royal Ulster Yacht Club on Seacliff Road for afternoon tea. The Duke of Edinburgh also took part in a special 120-yacht regatta in his Flying Fifteen "Cowslip." The Queen presented the awards, but her husband was not one of the winners.

Among the VIPs were Prime Minister Lord Brookeborough and Lady Brookeborough, Minister of Commerce Brian Faulkner, Minister of Home Affairs John Andrews, other Cabinet Ministers and local dignitaries.

Prince Charles and Princess Anne, who had enjoyed a picnic at Strangford, also visited Bangor en route to the Royal Yacht.

A section of the crowd awaiting the Queen's arrival at Bangor Castle in August 1961.
Spectator picture.

Security was minimal as Bangor well-wishers, many in hired rowing boats, witnessed the Queen's departure on the Royal barge at close proximity. Her Majesty can be seen waving (bottom right).
Spectator picture.

One of the leading campaigners for a major reconstruction project to transform the rapidly deteriorating Queen's Parade area was Royal Hotel owner Bill O'Hara. At a meeting of the Bangor Tourist Development Association on 6 October, he suggested a wall should be built from the Laird's Boats site near Pickie Pool across to the Central Pier.

The area within the wall, he said, could accommodate sunken gardens, paddling pools, a swimming pool and car parking. There was general agreement that if such a scheme were ever to happen, it would require a major injection of government funding, rather than the more limited local authority resources.

In November the Borough Council indicated it was considering four different sites for an indoor swimming pool and had instructed engineering consultants to prepare a report and submit preliminary estimates. The sites were at the gasworks stockyard (between Hamilton Road and Bingham Street); Ward Park, with a Hamilton Road frontage; between two of the town's three piers; and the front of Holborn Avenue (at the coastguard station).

The scene at upper Main Street as the crowd awaits the arrival of the Royal couple.
Spectator picture.

Lawrence Pitkethly

...remembers

Lawrence Pitkethly with his father Norman.

AFTER leaving the north of Ireland, Lawrence Pitkethly worked as a television journalist for the BBC's *Twenty Four Hours* and *Panorama*. At the same time he completed a Ph. D in French philosophy at the London School of Economics. He emigrated to the United States in 1973, where he taught cultural history at Hampshire College, Amherst, while continuing to write and direct films for the BBC. He then moved to New York where he wrote, directed and produced films for Public Broadcasting, mostly on cultural subjects.

He was executive producer for *Voices and Visions*, a 13-part series of films on American poets, which garnered *Time Magazine*'s accolade of 'Best cultural television series of 1988 on American television.' He followed that with directing a documentary film for Channel 4/UK and PBS on Russian poet Joseph Brodsky and executive producing a

THE waves at Ballyholme were wafer thin like the ice cream sliders we used to buy at Caproni's, rarely whipping up a lather for the yachts moored in the bay. As a boy I liked to roam the beach at low tide alone, or kick a football in the park until the light faded. On Saturdays when the weather was fine, my father and I would rent a row boat from Laird's, and we'd make for the end of the North Pier, where some of the supporting planks had rotted, permitting our craft to manoeuvre the crunching wavelets into a makeshift little grotto directly underneath the fishermen.

In those days, before the marina cut the bay off from the town, any oarsman had the run of the water; you could hug the shore at your ease, or head bravely towards the Lough until the strollers on Queen's Parade receded like specks.

Growing up in Bangor, in other words, was pretty idyllic for a kid; every summer day was an excursion. The town's perpetual holiday resort aura became more problematic for me as a teenager. Because I came from a strict religious family, normal adolescent haunts were off-limits, so I rarely glimpsed the inside of the Tonic Cinema, never went to the Fo'c'sle, nor to Caps for Saturday night dances, though I did occasionally sip coffee at the Calypso, a smoke-infested dive on upper Main Street, replete with plastic palm trees and a wall-poster for BOAC, featuring bullfighters.

My evangelical mother's tight rein on my activities set up a huge clash of interests, which I temporarily resolved by embarking on a brief stint as a boy preacher, at one point having a go, like the orators hawking God on the seafront, haranguing tourists, day trippers and local profligates from the Christian Workers stand at Pickie. This incendiary turn to my life may have seemed excessive to some onlookers, but it was a perfectly truthful resolution of tensions; and the rocket soon fizzled when I went to university in London. By the time I returned to the north of Ireland to work in BBC television as a presenter, I was no longer a zealot.

I also rediscovered Bangor's virtues. Every night I drove home to the same house on Groomsport Road where I had spent my boyhood. It's been torn down since, but in those days was a semi-detached with

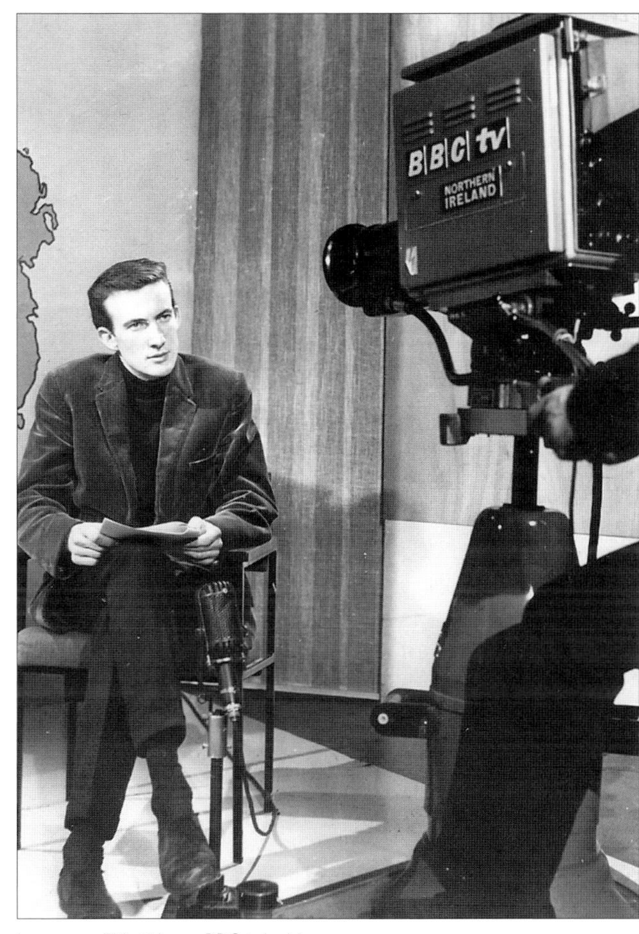

Lawrence Pitkethly on BBC television.
Picture courtesy of BBC Northern Ireland.

10-part series, *American Cinema,* in 1995 for PBS and BBC. In 2000 he wrote and co-directed *Belfast My Love*, a 90-minute on-camera, personal journey to Northern Ireland for RTE (Dublin) and ARTE (France).

He now resides in France and has devoted himself to writing – novels and non-fiction. A long poem of his, *Return of the Native*, was published in Ploughshares, Boston, edited by Derek Walcott, and he's recently completed a novel, *Loves of a Mother and Son*, set in Bangor. He's currently a Professor of Film at the American University of Paris. He has one daughter, Camille, born in 1992.

Lawrence with daughter Camille Pitkethly.

garden patch and welcoming hydrangeas at the front and back, sandwiched between St Columbanus church and Billy Simpson's garage. I often went to sleep lulled by the tide's distant susurrus or gulls screeching over the spire.

Some nights I took a detour round Seacliff Road to see the horn of the bay, or snuck down Sandringham to watch the Heysham and Liverpool steamers that passed down the Lough every evening like gleaming crates of lights; they were carrying their passengers on the first leg of a great voyage to far-off climes and cities. I'd hold my breath until the bracelets on the Antrim coast reappeared after a brief eclipse and the flare from the Larne lighthouse swivelled over the pitch-black water. There were more destinations in heaven and earth out there, and Bangor gave me the nudge to dream them.

1962

...the Spectator reports

Donna Douglas finished third in the United Kingdom's contest in February to select a song for the following month's Eurovision Song Contest in Luxembourg. Donna's "Message in a Bottle" was beaten by Belfast man Ronnie Carroll with "Ring-A-Ding Girl" and Australian Frank Ifield, runner-up with "Alone Too Long." Carroll finished fourth in the Eurovision final. Donna now lives in the Perth area of Western Australia.

Bangor Post Office drivers who received long service awards in early 1962. From left: Mr R. Hamilton, Mr J. F. Lisney (superintendent), Mr B. Duckworth, Mr J. Crompton, Mr H. Eddis (assistant inspector), Major J. H. Dougan, chairman of the Bangor Safety First Committee, Mr J. McManus (postmaster), Mr E. Hay, Mr W. Oughton (assistant head postmaster), Mr J. Moore (awarded a five-year medal), Mr W. Morrow, Mr E. Glithero and Mr J. Simpson. F. Totten, J. Boal, E. George and H. G. Orr, all award winners, missed the photo-call.
Spectator picture.

Receiving their sugar lumps at the Central Avenue health clinic: Joy, daughter of Mrs J. Redman, David and Timothy, sons of Mrs S. Spence, and Glenys, daughter of Mrs S. Harris. Included is health visitor Miss R. M. Morton. *Spectator* picture.

Bangor experienced a power cut on Wednesday 21 February, just as the BBC was about to broadcast a recording of John Glenn's historic spaceflight in *Friendship 7*, during which he became the first American to orbit the Earth. This prompted Bangor postman Ernie Glithero, of 15 Park Avenue, to query whether there was "a communist element among our electricity staff."

In a letter to the *Spectator* he wrote: "I've noticed it several times when anything of interest is about to happen, we have a power cut. Roll on the day when someone invents a gas-operated TV set."

Oral vaccination for polio through sugar lumps and syrup was introduced in Bangor for the first time in April. Figures showed that 10 per cent of children aged between six months and 15 years were not being immunised against poliomyelitis, which was deemed a "treacherous, dangerous and deadly disease."

Bangor's new automatic telephone exchange came into operation on 12 April, giving subscribers complete dialling access within a 20-mile radius. Plans were

Bangor telephone exchange operators who lost their jobs to automation in April 1962. From left: Mrs M. M. Harrison, Mrs M. L. Rutherford, Miss J. A. Gilmore, Mrs C. E. McConachy (assistant supervisor), Miss M. J. Bewley, Miss M. E. Green, Miss L. W. Watson, Miss J. L. Murray and Miss M. A. Gorman.
Spectator picture.

also announced for calls without operator assistance to leading cross-channel cities within a year.

"The march of progress and automation seldom leaves humans unscathed," reported the *Spectator*. "All the local operators will go, depriving us of the personal touch forever on all but trunk calls and other such services."

To launch the new automatic service, Mayor Charles Valentine made the first call to Mrs Kathleen Hadow, of Seacourt, the first person to have a telephone connected to a Bangor exchange (at Southwell Road) back in 1903. For nearly 60 years her number was '1' but in 1962 it became '5001.'

Messrs John Lightbody, Grocer and Restaurateur, of 7/9 Main Street, closed on 28 April after 81 years in business. For 65 of those years Mr Robert Lightbody had worked in the family firm and the closure also marked his retirement.

The premises were subsequently purchased for £40,000 by the Belfast Co-Operative Society. When added to their existing premises at the foot of Main Street, along with the business of Messrs Robert Neill and Sons at 15/21 Main Street, which they had also acquired, it gave the Co-Op an extensive frontage measuring some 126ft. The entire site was redeveloped into an ultra-modern department store, which opened in May 1964.

Also in April, electrical and furniture dealer Mr H. Cowan sold his premises at 35 Main Street to Lipton's for £20,000. They revealed plans to rebuild the property as a supermarket, while Mr Cowan moved to High Street.

On Monday 28 May Bangor's new £68,000 police station, built on the site of a former nursery school on the approach road to Bangor Castle, came into operation. One of the most modern and best equipped stations in the province, the complex included two substantial dwellings to the rear, occupied by Sgts. McKeown and (Jack) Hermon and their families.

Moving into the new police station on the approach road to Bangor Castle. *Spectator* picture.

The police station was previously located in two houses at Victoria Road. Strangers to the town often couldn't find it and the premises provided little comfort or convenience for their occupants.

Removing firearms (and a bicycle) from the former police premises at Victoria Road. *Spectator* picture.

Guest of honour that same day at Trinity Presbyterian Church was Miss Jennie Hanna MBE, who, by then in her 83rd year, had been superintendent of the Church Street Mission Hall since 1898. She received a wrist watch from the women who attended Monday afternoon meetings in the hall that Miss Hanna still conducted. The gift was actually handed over on their behalf by 78-year-old John Halliday, who, as a boy, had been a member of the volunteer team responsible for building the hall.

The Rev. J. T. Carson said she was "friendly and down to earth, so completely human, showing the gospel is not just about something in the sky alone."

Plans for a new hotel at Clandeboye received a mixed reception in June, when discussed at a meeting of North Down Rural Council. The planners objected to the proposal because the site was within a green belt area with high visual amenities. The soil was of "exceptionally high agricultural value" and the planners felt it should be "kept from non-agricultural development." Councillors, however, determined there was an urgent need for first-class hotels in the district.

The camera resulted in a variety of expressions during play in the playground of debretta's Bangor factory. In front—William Martin, Karen McFarland, Sharon Martin. In background—David Brown, Sandra Brown, Noel McLarnon and (with Mrs. C. Patton) Evelyn Adams. Donna Patton is on the climbing frame, and in centre of picture is Mrs. P. Woods. Missing from photograph—Terence Beattie (22 months) and Deborah Cree (19 months).
"Spectator" Photo. AF 25.

In the same month Bangor's biggest employer, the Debretta factory on the Clandeboye Road, introduced a crèche for women among its 250-strong workforce with children under school age. Nurse Christine Patton and assistant

Pearl Woods were on hand, for a payment of £1 a week per child, to look after them during the working day.

Belfast businessmen Trevor Kane and Dermot O'Donnell paid £50,000 for the 60-bedroom Ship Hotel on Queen's Parade. Their plans for the renamed Queen's Court Hotel included an end to public dancing – the last was the "Miss Bangor Football" final on 22 June, which was won by 19-year-old Ann Gavin, from Hillcrest in the town.

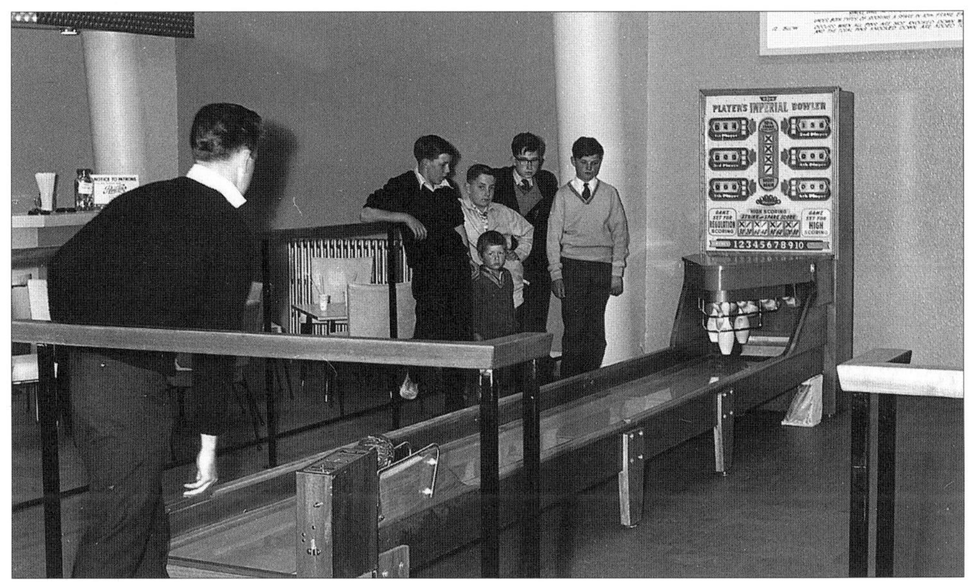

George Nelson, of Grovehill Gardens, Bangor, tries his hand at one of the new Imperial Bowls alleys in the Tonic Cinema. *Spectator* picture.

A new attraction arrived at the Tonic Cinema in July with the introduction of "the gripping game of Imperial Bowls" – miniature alleys featuring "flashing lights on a seemingly complicated coloured scoreboard, the crash as the bowl hits the skittles and the whirr as the bowl is returned to the player." An initial three lanes in the former upstairs restaurant quickly doubled to six, along with a further three in the shop to the left of the Tonic entrance.

TONIC : BANGOR
Phone 5830
It's here ! : It's here !
SOMETHING NEW IN ENTERTAINMENT !
IMPERIAL BOWLS
THE LATEST GAME OF SKILL
OPENING MONDAY, 9th JULY
Also for your added pleasure—The Theatre
MODERN SNACK BAR
will be open daily from 10 a.m.

Hopes were raised among enthusiasts that if the game proved popular enough, a full-sized automatic 10-pin bowling alley would be installed at the Tonic. However, numbers gradually dwindled and the Imperial Bowls equipment was removed the following year.

On 2 August estate agent Brian Wimpress became the youngest member of Bangor Borough Council after he defeated former Councillor Harry E. Grindle by just 19 votes (676 to 657) in a by-election for the Castle Ward. Mr Wimpress was the first official Liberal candidate to contest a local government election in Bangor. His Unionist opponent was grocery manager with Messrs. Smyth and McClure.

Mourne granite foundation stones were laid on 8 September for the new £100,000 West Church at Crawfordsburn Road. One of the stones bore the name of the minister, the Rev. David Bailie, "thus connecting his name with the church for posterity."

The scene at Ballyholme following the robbery.
Spectator picture.

The 'Great Ballyholme Pepper Robbery' took place at lunchtime on 6 November, when a well-dressed man entered the Groomsport Road sub-branch of the Belfast Banking Co. Ltd. He struck the sole occupant, officer-in-charge Charles A. Radcliffe, on the head with a walking stick and temporarily blinded him by throwing pepper in his face.

Mr and Mrs Charles Radcliffe at home after the bank robbery.
Spectator picture.

Quickly on the scene were two local shopkeepers, Messrs J. M. McQuoid and Richard McCartney, as well as butcher's assistant Robert Whitla, from Eddie Mills' adjoining butcher's shop, who alerted the police. Officers arrived within minutes but the culprit had made good his escape with £300 in cash. Cars on every road in the area were stopped and a police dog joined officers for a search on foot.

Mr Radcliffe worked alone in the peaceful outlying part of the town "and it was clear the robbery had been planned meticulously and executed with cold-blooded callousness," reported the *Spectator*. It was the only recorded bank robbery in Bangor during the Sixties.

These Bangor firemen took part in a large-scale training exercise in the early 1960s. From left: Leading Fireman Roy Emerson, Firemen Percy Marshall, George Whyte, John Gore, Jimmy McAuley and Leading Fireman Frankie Millsopp. *Spectator* picture.

Long service and good conduct medals were presented to Leading Fireman Frankie Millsopp, of the Bangor Section of the Northern Ireland Fire Authority, on 16 November. He had joined the Auxiliary Fire Service in 1941 serving with distinction to the end of the Second World War. In 1946 Mr Millsopp became a Retained Fireman on the creation of the NIFA.

Bangor's oldest established business, coal merchant Robert Neill and Sons, moved into new premises at 137 Main Street on 26 November. It was only their third address in an unbroken history stretching back more than 150 years. Previously they had been located at 7 Sandy Row (near the Queen's Cinema) and, after 1931, at 19 Main Street.

Long-standing staff members in 1962 included Hugh Moore (45 years), Samuel McClements (42 years), Andrew Lightbody (40), Wilfred J. Reynolds (38), Miss Maureen Sayers (34), John Robinson (34), William Wilson (34), Francis McGlennon (33) and Walter Reid (32).

Broadcaster Rose Neill is a fifth generation member of the family.

Raymond Fox
...remembers

Raymond Fox and future wife Jean Moore in 1965.

CANON Raymond Fox served as an apprentice at Short Brothers and Harland, 1962-69; Curate, Holywood Parish, 1971-75; Minor Canon, Down Cathedral, and RE teacher, Down High School, 1975-78; Rector of Killinchy Union, 1978-81; Rector of St. Mary's, Crumlin Road, Belfast, 1981-88; Rector, Chaplain, Belvoir Park Hospital, and Rural Dean, Carryduff, 1988-2000; Canon, Down Cathedral, 1998-2000; Canon, Belfast Cathedral, 2000-02; Rector and Rural Dean, Donegal Town Group of Parishes, 2002 to present; Canon, Raphoe Cathedral, 2009. Married to Jean (née Moore of Bangor) on 14 March 1970; children: Suzanne, Alison and Michael.

AS 1970 dawned I was on the threshold of ordination. Being brought up in Bangor post-Second World War, I had known nothing about restricted education opportunities, poor housing or any lack of employment possibilities.

I'm so thankful for every encouragement I was given in the late 1950s and early 1960s. My family couldn't do enough for my brother and me. Bangor Tech enabled people like me, who had not sat the 11-Plus, to gain exam results on the science and practical side. It was a place for results. In the final year contacts were made with the engineering firms and many of us had multiple choices as to where we started work.

I was heavily involved in church activities. I was in both the 2nd and 6th Boys' Brigade Companies. Eddie Miley was my role model. I was a Northern Ireland representative at a BB International Camp at Glenalmond, near Perth, Scotland. Membership also gave opportunities through the annual July camp to get away on holiday. Friendships were cemented at the camps.

At the same time Hamilton Road Methodist Church ran an excellent Youth Guild. Gus Addy was my role model. On Sunday evenings we had discussions about topics such as "telling the truth", euthanasia, boy/girl relationships and, of course, in a church setting, what it meant to be a follower of Jesus.

Raymond Fox, of Second Bangor Company Boys' Brigade, receiving the Queen's Badge from his mother Molly. Looking on is the Captain, Mr Dick Beattie. *Spectator* picture.

I was involved in both Bangor Parish and Bangor Abbey. George Quin was my hero, as well as curates Raymond Hay and Robin Eames. I was a Parish Youth Representative in discussions regarding a renewed church, through the report "Administration 67". Bangor Parish also had a Sunday night group, the Youth Forum, which went around people's houses. Bill Patterson was my role model.

Back in 1963, Raymond Fox and Robert Walker, 6th Bangor BB, welcomed the New Zealand contingent to Bangor on their way to the BB International Camp in Scotland. *Spectator* picture.

With my peers in the local churches we set up the Bangor Ecumenical Youth Council. Fr Murray encouraged Catholic young people to be involved.

I spent time at Pickie Pool. Andy Johnston was my role model. I took part in square dancing and walked in the Mournes. Although I never did the Mourne Wall Walk, I still have a map showing that over a period I climbed every peak. We had really enjoyable times. Only once were we ever washed out.

The Sixties was an era of expansion of the population. This gave rise to new church buildings. I can remember being part of a group with Edward Darling to see St. Gall's church being built. A number of churches were built around the "new" Bangor, the Church of Ireland also building at the Primacy and Kilcooley. All these congregations were to make a significant contribution to social cohesion for people coming to live in Bangor.

A window to the outside world came through Christian Aid, the development agency. Marsden Fitzsimons was my role model. He helped us organise church services and get a shop on Main Street each year to have a display. During this time I met Jean Moore, later to become Mrs Fox.

Canon Raymond Fox today. Picture courtesy of Jason McGarrigle.

The early Sixties saw me start work in Shorts, the aircraft factory. They encouraged day release and this led me to Trade Scholarships and on to Queen's to study Engineering. From Queen's I was accepted to train for Ordination in Trinity. I had the joy of being made Deacon in Bangor Parish and ordained priest in Bangor Abbey.

The Sixties for me represented opportunities in education, church and recreational activities.

Raymond Fox (centre) with members of the Methodist Youth Guild at Easter 1965 in the Cairngorms.

1963

...the Spectator reports

Many would argue that for the teenagers of Bangor the Sixties started on Saturday morning, 5 January 1963, the day the Tonic hosted its first TTS – Tonic Teenage Show. Bangor had always had its youth groups, such as the Scouts and Guides, Boys' and Girls' Brigades, as well as numerous other church-based organisations, but this was different and was a clear reflection of changing times. Hosted by Tonic manager Capt. Alec Jones, the doors opened at 10.15am and admission was just 1/3d. The TTS featured guest performers, some of them semi-professional, a host of talented young people, record requests and a "Way to the Stars" talent competition – young saxophonist Van Morrison supposedly among the early contestants. Such a radical development was not to everyone's liking. Mrs M. Greenfield, of 18 Seacliff Road,

TEENAGE PANEL OFF TO GOOD START

FOLLOWING on the success of the Teenage Record Panel on shows like "Thank Your Lucky Stars" and "Preview" on T.V., the T.T.S. Panel got off to a good start on Saturday morning.

With Richard Morrow, assisted by Colin Barnes, doing a grand job in the chairman's chair, the three teenagers, two from the audience and one from the show, gave their opinions on three of the latest waxings.

If future panelists can follow the example set by Saturday's trio, then this latest T.T.S. innovation is in for a long run.

Heather Hawthorne, Bertie Niblock (from the audience), and Brian Taylor, were clearly spoken and intelligent in all they said about each disc. Well done, and congratulations all round!

wrote in a letter to the *Spectator*: "Nowadays it's difficult enough for teenagers to pass all their examinations and to do their jobs properly. Teenagers are not adults, they are very young people who want to enjoy life, and they will not resist if you offer them amusement all the time... There are enough young people in show business already, especially singers, setting very often bad examples."

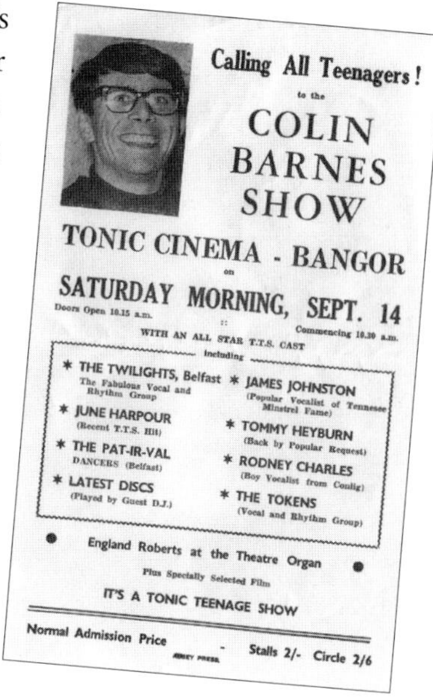

Bangor was hit by the first of several spells of exceptionally bad weather, thereby creating the "big freeze-up" of early 1963. A blizzard arrived during the early hours of Sunday morning 20 January. Snow on overhead wires caused short-circuiting, resulting in a breakdown in the power supply to several parts of the town.

Although traffic moved quite freely, country roads proved difficult to negotiate. Buses and trains operated as normally as possible, but for children it was fun all the way – with any suitable hill proving popular for tin tray sleigh rides.

A second blizzard on Tuesday 5 February proved more troublesome, with the *Spectator* describing it as "the worst in living memory." All roads out of Bangor were impassable, there were frequent power losses, many schoolchildren were sent home, and there were shortages of bread and milk. The town was virtually isolated by snowdrifts and many shops were forced to close.

Mr A. Lockwood and young son Stephen managed to complete their milk round by using a sleigh, in this instance to negotiate their way up the Brunswick Road.
Spectator picture.

In response to the instant success of the Tonic Teenage Show, the *Spectator* launched its first young people's section, penned by 25-year-old linotype operator John Gore. It included regular performance reviews and Hit Parade charts

Enjoying the snow on the hills at Bangor Golf Club.
Spectator picture.

comparing Bangor's Top 10 with the UK chart.

One of his earliest reviews praised Phil Coulter and the Glee Men following their TTS appearance on 16 March. After hearing their charity single "Foolin' Time," along with an instrumental called "Thunderbird," John wrote: "These boys certainly have talent to write and record a disc of such quality – all on their own."

The bleak scene at upper Main Street.
Spectator picture.

The Rev Ian Paisley, addressing a meeting on 15 March in the King's Hall at Central Avenue, held under the auspices of the Bangor Women's White Ribboners, criticised Bangor Protestants for permitting Jesus to be portrayed as a doll in a crib at the town's Christmas tree, the local Borough Council for deciding to open sports grounds on Sundays, and the Bangor Council of Churches for being affiliated to the World Council of Churches, which had the Pope's support.

Ivan Pollin and John Crowe, owners of Romanos in Belfast, announced plans on 10 May to replace the former Astor Cinema on Seacliff Road with a new ballroom, costing between £90,000 and £120,000, to be named Milanos.

On 7 June Mary Peters, tipped as a strong contender for the pentathlon at the 1964 Tokyo Olympics, joined Bangor Athletics Club at the invitation of coach Richard Weglarz to help re-establish the ladies section.

On 8 August, and using a bulldozer rather than a spade, Mayor Charles F. Milligan cut the first sod to start work on the new ring road, connecting the Newtownards and Bloomfield Roads.

It was revealed on 23 August that some 100,000 British and Irish coins, mainly pennies, had been donated to Guide Dogs for the Blind through a specially constructed slot in the window of the Ex-Service Club premises on High Street. They were converted into a cheque for £750, which was presented to the charity by the club's president, blind ex-Serviceman Cllr Bertie McConnell, who was accompanied by faithful guide dog Rena.

Bertie McConnell with guide dog Rena.
Spectator picture.

John Pringle in his 1963 Cooper Climax, which had a top speed of 184mph.
Spectator picture.

A Bangor link to the £2.6m Great Train Robbery was revealed to the town's Rotary Club, when local garage owner John Pringle told fellow members he had met Roy James, one of the men still being sought in connection with the 8 August robbery. Mr Pringle had met James at a pre-race practice in Dublin's Phoenix Park on 26 July. The Main Street businessman drove a Cooper, while James had a Brabham. The man he later realised was James told Mr Pringle, when asked his occupation, that he was a "professional burglar" and that it was an "excellent profession."

The *Spectator* of 20 September reported that new film *The Longest Day* had very real meaning for Mr Robert Poole, who worked in Bertie Mawhinney's barber's shop on Queen's Parade. In the film Major John Howard (played by Richard Todd), of the 2nd Battalion Oxford and Bucks Light Infantry, leads a glider attack by the 6th Airborne Division on bridges in Normandy as part of the D-Day operations.

Among those in the real Major Howard's glider back in June 1944 was Robert Poole. Altogether two platoons of D Company and two of the RUR made the glider landing and successfully captured the targets.

The North Down Hospitals Management Committee, meeting on 28 September, decided that visitors to Bangor Hospital would be banned from smoking anywhere in the buildings, while patients would be limited to certain times of the day.

Consultant Surgeon Mr Alexander Calder said he had gone into a general ward after visiting time to see a patient "and thought there was a fire." He added: "You could not see the other end of the ward. Apart from that, the floor was littered with burnt cigarette butts."

It wasn't until October 1968 that the committee terminated a long-standing rental agreement for cigarette machines inside the hospital, including one in the X-Ray department's waiting room.

Terry Neill was joined on the Northern Ireland team by another Bangor man, Linfield left-back John Parke, for a 2-1 home victory over Scotland on Saturday 12 October. Within weeks the Silverstream Drive man had signed for Scottish club Hibernian for £12,500.

Local organisations paid tribute to President John F. Kennedy, assassinated in Dallas, Texas, on 22 November 1963. Speaking on behalf of the Aldermen, Councillors and townspeople of Bangor, Mayor Milligan extended "to all Americans living in our midst our heartfelt sympathy." He added: "We were all deeply shocked at the occurrence and join with our friends in mourning the loss of a great President, who endeared himself to the people of Ireland when, earlier this year, he visited the land of his forefathers."

BANGOR MEMORY – Taylor's Garage at the High Street junction with the Ballyholme Road in the early 1960s.

Brian Frazer
...remembers

BRIAN Frazer left Bangor Grammar School after gaining the Senior Certificate in June 1962. However, that same October he contracted Pleurisy and entered Forster Green Hospital. He was discharged in April 1963. In September 1963 he worked as a Costing Clerk for J. E. Coulter Ltd (Ford Agents), of Chichester Street, Belfast. He entered the Weights and Measures Department of the Civil Service (present day Trading Standards Department) in 1964, and eventually passed his Board of Trade exams, qualifying as an Inspector.

In July 1965, at the age of 20, he married and, in time, was promoted to Divisional Inspector and transferred to Armagh in 1972. He divorced in 1977/8 and resigned from the Civil Service, subsequently joining the RUC in August 1978. Three years later he remarried and moved back to Bangor (living within a mile of where he was born).

IT wasn't that I didn't like girls, it was just that so much of my life was taken up with outdoor pursuits like fishing and shooting and exploring the local surroundings, that being in female company came second in importance to my main interests. Besides, although I found them fascinating, I was always a bit "in awe" of the fair sex and unsure of myself.

For a start, my hair would not comb in the "DA" style of the time (probably because my mother always instructed the barber to make sure the parting was to the left), and I never thought of myself as attractive to the opposite sex. There was one beauty I absolutely worshipped, and who just took my breath away when I was near her. She never knew how I felt. All I will say is that she lived in Grovehill Gardens.

In between seeing how far we could get up Jenny Watt's Cave (just past Seacourt on the coastal path), or exploring the underground bunkers at the gun emplacements at Ballymacormick Point, or organising an expedition up the river that flowed out at Queen's Parade (underneath the Gasworks and up to Ward Park), my time was spent "over the fields." On more than one Monday I was called to account for my absence from Bangor Grammar School's rugby match

Brian Frazer on 8 October 1962 – two days before he entered hospital. The picture was taken at the junction of Castle Lane and Donegall Place in Belfast by a street photographer just after Brian's great uncle, Jack Stuart, had bought him a new shotgun for his birthday.

Brian served in the RUC until his retirement in 1999, spending his final nine years as a Sergeant Instructor in the Training Centre at Garnerville. He is now living the "out to grass" life with his wife and three children (two boys and a girl). He hopes to enjoy as many more years as possible, playing snooker (badly), strumming his 12-string guitar (badly), drinking a glass of red wine or vodka (with expertise), and having as few "senior moments" as time will allow!

the previous Saturday morning, having been selected to play for one of the teams.

Unfortunately the outcome of my outdoor activities and many soakings was that I contracted Pleurisy not long after leaving school in 1962, and ended up in Forster Green Hospital in October of that year, a week after my 18th birthday. It was devastating to me and my family, but a major turning point in my life.

The approved treatment in a TB hospital at that time, in addition to prescribed drugs, was plenty of good fresh air and, in recovery, the policy was to let patients get up and about in increasing amounts of time, most of it spent outdoors in turntable shelters with adjustable beds and mattresses.

The hospital staff were absolutely brilliant. One lady in particular, who was really good to me, was a Mrs Morrison and she looked after me like a son. It was a few years later that I discovered she was the mother of Van himself!

We, the patients, organised all the everyday things ourselves, like newspaper deliveries, morning and evening, recreational activities, including film shows on Wednesday, Rec. nights with table tennis, snooker competitions, and our own hospital radio request programme, through our internal radio system. I made many great friends and I also met my first wife (who was another patient) in Forster Green Hospital. It was a complete chapter of my life.

The winter of 62/63 was incredible. Freezing temperatures and snow 3ft deep for months on end. How the rest of the country survived I don't know, but in our wee world our main concern was that the "Film Man" would make it through the snow so we could get a "snog" in the back row of the Rec. room during the film.

Emerging into the "real world" in April 1963 was a bit of a shock. Six months is not a long time, but as a teenager it is a lifetime. So much had changed!

From the start of the "Singing Pubs" and the Clancy Brothers, Dubliners, etc., it was now more of a professional scene. Groups like The Sapphires, The Janitors, Salt Water Brig, etc. had taken over. Acts like Tommy Heyburn and Anne and Jack Chambers had emerged. There were now so many more places to go, for example the Queen's Court Hotel (with really big stars like Engelbert Humperdinck, Frank Ifield, etc.), The Windsor, The Warwick, The Royal and later Milanos.

My Dad and great friend sadly died in 1965 at the young age of 55, and I still miss him to this day. I was married at 20 in July of the same year (too young), which again sadly didn't last long.

If I had the chance I would love to go through it all again, but I would make a lot of changes. I would tell a lot of people what I never had a chance to tell them (or was too afraid). I would not follow through hasty decisions.

Yes, the Sixties – they were something else!

Brian Frazer just before his retirement from the RUC.

Winners of the principal awards at a sports day when Brian was still a student at Bangor Grammar School. Back row (from left): N. McManus, M. D. Mason, H. D. McCutcheon, M. Affolter and N. S. Alexander. Middle row (from left): C. R. Beattie, B. B. Powell, D. M. R. Gorman, J. G.Tinsley and J. Frazer. Front: Brian Frazer and G. Beattie. *Spectator* picture.

1964

...the Spectator reports

Bangor's first ever woman Councillor, Mrs Jean Levine, resigned her seat in February as she and husband Alex were leaving Northern Ireland. Mrs Levine, who had arrived in Bangor 25 years earlier from her native Scotland, had represented the Clifton Ward since winning a by-election in 1957.

The town's first Chinese restaurant, the Ambassador, opened in March on the site of the former Milan Restaurant on High Street. Proprietor was 30-year-old Kiu Cheung Lam.

Bangor bus conductor Tony Mulligan, of 54 Grovehill Gardens, had particular interest in *Thank Your Lucky Stars* broadcast on 18 April. It featured Liverpool band The Merseybeats and his nephew Tony Crane was their vocalist and lead guitarist.

Bangor was chosen in April by the Milk Marketing Board for the launch of its latest product – yoghurt. "It is available from many of Bangor's grocers today and most will be staging demonstrations of the many ways of preparing it for serving," ran an advertising feature in the *Spectator*.

The redevelopment of the Castle Street/ Castle Square area saw the oldest residents, William (80) and Hugh Mawhinney (70) and their sister Mrs Mary Miskelly, moving to Lisadell Drive. The family had lived at No 54 for 69 years, with Mrs Miskelly commenting: "I think I'm going to like it. It's going to be better for our health."

Another resident of Castle Square, Henry McDaid, who had lived there all his 57 years, also moved to Lisadell Drive. The former Merchant Navy cook faced a new weekly rent of £2. 2s. 9d, compared to just 13/7d.

The Bangor Ratepayers' Association scored a 100 per cent success in the May Borough Council elections. Beryl Holland (Ballyholme), Alexander Baird (Dufferin) and George Storey (Princetown) were all poll toppers, while their other success was achieved by Ernest Uprichard (Clifton).

Cllr Beryl Holland.

The *Spectator* of 29 May reported that the Tonic Teenage Show would close on 6 June. It had been suffering from declining audiences, prompting *Spectator* reporter Helen Russell to comment: "All the enthusiasm and vigour has died and there must be very few who will be sorry to see it go, as far as entertainment is concerned."

Bangor Grammar School headmaster Randall Clarke hit the headlines at the end of June after declaring, in end of term reports to parents, that strict hairstyle regulations were necessary.

"I believe boys should be allowed some latitude to express their individual tastes," he wrote. "Unfortunately, some have 'let their hair down' to an

Facing the prospect of a "short back and sides" before the start of the 1964/65 school year were (from left): Stephen Collins, Tony Roberts and Peter Murgatroyd.
Spectator picture.

unbecoming extent and what started as a mild eccentricity among a few has developed into an infectious craze, which is even affecting some intelligent boys.

"It is obviously time to stop this fashion from continuing as a distracting nuisance in school life. From the beginning of the September term boys must have the traditional 'short back and sides' haircut and will not be admitted to school unless they have it."

The 4 September edition of the *Spectator* reported: "It was a somewhat shorn mass, who congregated in the school assembly hall on the first morning. Three young gentlemen were asked to go home and see to it they had the regulation carried out before the following morning.

"No doubt among the boys these young Rolling Stones were the heroes of the day, but alas they are no longer, for the headmaster is satisfied that each and everybody has been coiffured according to the rule."

Bangor Lions Club was formed in September, with Hal McGimpsey serving as founder president. Fortnightly meetings were held in the Royal Hotel.

A £170,000 extension at Bangor Hospital, which doubled the number of beds available, was opened on 29 September by Lord Wakehurst, Governor of Northern Ireland. The *Spectator* described it as "the start of a new era of hospital services in Bangor, representing 10 years of thought, planning, arguing, wrangling, and wrestling with technical difficulties."

Mayor Milligan unveiled two half-crown stamp vending machines in October to help people facing difficulty paying their rates. One was located outside the gas offices in High Street and the other was on the Belfast Bank wall at the Hamilton Road corner. Stamps were stuck into special booklets, each holding up to £30 worth, which could go towards paying a rates bill.

The first section of the ring road, from the Newtownards Road to Bloomfield Road, was opened by Health and Local Government Minister William Craig on 23 October. The Council refused applications from Regent Oil, Shell Mex and BP for sites adjoining the new road for petrol stations. It was felt there was ample space on the main approach roads.

Beatles Paul, Ringo, John and George with Bangor-based promoter Trevor Kane (second from left) and John Fanning, from NEMS (the group's management company).
Spectator picture.

PUBLIC NOTICES

BRIAN EPSTEIN and ARTHUR HOWES
in conjunction with TREVOR KANE and GEORGE CONNELL present

THE BEATLES

AND FULL SUPPORTING PROGRAMME

KING'S HALL, BELFAST

MONDAY, 2ND NOVEMBER AT 8.45 P.M.

TICKETS—20/-, 15/-, 10/- (Reserved) and 7/6 (Unreserved)

ON SALE THIS SATURDAY AT DUNDONALD, NEWTOWNARDS and CROSSGAR; also at GEORGE CONNELL, BOOKING OFFICE, 39 HIGH STREET, BELFAST, and by post from TREVOR KANE PROMOTIONS, 149 KING'S ROAD, BELFAST (send stamped addressed envelope and Cheque or Postal Order)

Queen's Court Hotel owner Trevor Kane and colleague George McConnell concluded negotiations to bring The Beatles to the King's Hall in Belfast on 2 November at a cost of £10,000. Mr Kane described the discussions for the group's only appearance in Ireland in 1964, as "the toughest I have ever known."

QUEEN'S HALL NEWTOWNARDS
This Saturday 8—11.30 6/-
GREAT DOUBLE ATTRACTION
KINGS with PRINCE VINCE (Dublin)
THEM Stars of "THANK YOUR LUCKY STARS" "READY STEADY GO," etc.

Milanos BANGOR
IRELAND'S NEWEST LUXURY BALLROOM
OPENING TO-NIGHT (FRIDAY)
WITH THE FABULOUS
MIAMI SHOWBAND 9—1
AND THE MELOTONES
Sat., 12th 8—12 THE CADETS AND THE MELOTONES

Milanos opened on 11 December with the Miami Showband topping the bill. Acts appearing in the following months included The Searchers, Julie Rogers, Dusty Springfield, Brian Poole and the Tremeloes, Joe Brown, the Everly Brothers and The Kinks.

Bangor Borough Council vetoed a plan in December to create an eight-foot wide concrete "marine highway" from Ballyholme to Groomsport, via Ballymacormick Point. Councillors decided it would "spoil the amenities of the area."

Appearing on New Year's Eve at rhythm 'n' blues 'rave' the Crypt in Ward Park – the pavilion beside the bowling green – was Belfast band Them. Within weeks the group, featuring lead singer Van Morrison, were in the UK's Top 10 with "Baby Please Don't Go."

Date for New Year's Eve

WHY not see the New Year in at the Crypt with "Them" who are making their first appearance in Bangor? At this rhythm and blues rave in the Ward Park Pavilion there will be dancing from 8 p.m. till 1 a.m. "The Sapphires," hosts for the evening, will also be introducing "The Dimensions." So come on, all you rhythm and blues fans, and make it a date.

The usually quiet setting of the Ward Park bowling green with the pavilion in the background – venue for one night only for an appearance by Them with Van Morrison on New Year's Eve 1964.
Spectator picture.

David Montgomery
...remembers

Spectator picture.

DAVID Montgomery attended Bangor Grammar School from 1960-67 and Queen's University, Belfast, from 1967-70, graduating with a BA in History and Politics. He joined the Mirror Group as a graduate trainee, then worked for the *Daily Mirror* and *Sunday Mirror* as a sub-editor/ chief sub-editor/ production editor in Manchester and London. He was chief sub-editor of *The Sun* between 1980 and 1982, before becoming Assistant Editor of the *Sunday People* in 1982 and Editor of the *News of the World* between 1985 and 1987.

As managing director of News UK Ltd. he acquired *Today* from the Lonrho group and managed its standalone operation as Editor until its integration with *The Sun* and *News of the World* in 1991. Between 1992 and 1999 David was chief executive of the Mirror Group, overseeing its restructuring and including the acquisitions of Midland Independent Newspapers plc,

PERHAPS we were still Blues Unlimited, a contradiction in terms as we were severely limited, or maybe by then had evolved into The Power & The Glory, the name that mortally offended my church-going mother's sense of decorum.

Anyway, my sole claim to popular music fame is for my blues band to have played the 'break' for Them in the Ward Park bowling pavilion sometime in the mid-Sixties while I was still at Bangor Grammar School. To this day in my mind's eye I see Van the Man standing next to me in the pavilion urinals, his long matted hair then a wonder to behold before the hat was donned in later life.

In Bangor, in the Sixties, anything was possible for grammar school boys who grew up with a sense of freedom and independence, despite the outwardly rather strait-laced society with its pretensions of middle class gentility. The advancing free spirit of the era, accompanied by the freedom and safety to roam from a very tender age and a classical piano education bestowed by my parents, equipped me for my short-lived pop career.

I could pontificate about Bangor in the 1960s as the most anglicised part of the east of Northern Ireland, snobbishly shrugging off the Irish showband tradition, even if it was merely substituted by an anaemic offshoot of the 'Belfast beat' blues scene.

But participation in the liberated Sixties was a foregone conclusion for our Bangor generation and that, and the coming Ulster Troubles, shattered the idyllic calm of a near heavenly childhood unique to that time.

I write this looking across an acre of communal gardens outside the back door of my home in central London. This is the confine of my eight-year-old son's domain and how I sometimes wish that I was bringing him up in Bangor, where our territory at a not much older age stretched from Groomsport to Helen's Bay. For us it was an adventure playground of beaches and hidden coves for whole days spent away from home with even cautious parents knowing that people would 'look out for us.'

Our nearest hang-out to home was what we called the 'Big Hole' – Ballyholme people naturally preferred the more elegant 'Long Hole' – where we used limpets as bait for crabs.

Innocent pleasures abounded, but Bible class and two church services on Hamilton Road on Sunday was a reminder that we were not put on earth for fun, although Bangor did its best to dispute that and I fear this diligent devotion did not keep me on the straight and narrow, either.

Sentimental it may be but over the decades of Ulster's torment Bangor and other places like it, where decency and a good quality of life persisted, could be pointed to as representing hope.

Of course the simple pleasures of pre-adolescence gave way to the tingling of glamour and excitement as other attractions went on parade. Summer on Queen's Parade, had I known it then a fair representation of the Italian *passeggiata*, awakened more complicated sentiments. And like Italy it was as much about the young men showing off their Turtle-waxed chassis on interminable circuits down Gray's Hill and along the

David Montgomery today.

Independent Newspapers plc, the (Belfast) *News Letter* and the *Derry Journal*, a 20% stake in Scottish Media Group plc and *The Racing Post*.

He is now chief executive of Mecom, which he founded in 2000 and was its executive chairman until January 2009. It is a European content and consumer business. The Group owns over 300 printed titles and over 200 websites in its four divisions, with substantial operations in the Netherlands, Denmark, Norway and Poland, together with a readership of 20 million per week and attracting 24 million unique website users per month.

Parade as it was the girls – mostly 'visitors' as we called them – showing off their more, to my mind, desirable bodies.

The spectator sport involved perching on the sea wall as it was then, hoping that something miraculous might happen with us boys practising chat-up lines on each other rather than trying them out for real. But Bangor then had not really emerged from a society in which anything remotely pleasurable was sinful.

Sin was about at least on a weekly basis with the temptation of Saturday night at the Duckpond – I think we called it a hop, a case of over-optimism as standing up at the end of the evening was enough of a challenge. Yes, Ward Park was quite a den of iniquity and the emphasis was less on dancing and more on the teenage consumption of as much as possible sherry, cider and beer of now long lost brands – was one Merrydown? – or they should be.

With teenage children today the dreary conclusion must be that society has not moved on much except theirs is champagne.

Then, it was largely a healthy childhood and teenage years in an environment adorned with natural beauty, along the coast stretching to the drumlins of Strangford for the boy cyclist on long evenings. Tomatoes and lettuce were eaten only from June to September as whatever came locally and in season, herrings off the boat included, was accepted and that has left an indelible preference on my diet in later life.

Another seemingly trifling incident from Bangor, and a first memory of home in Victoria Drive, left a more critical imprint on my emotional DNA. When we were pre-school I played with twins with red hair a few doors away. When primary school beckoned these boys disappeared from my life for ever. They turned one way to walk to school and I another. When Bangor contemporaries of whichever persuasion, now living away, speak of a similar experience they describe it as having been deprived of the society of the other half of the community.

After four decades I know this has changed for today's children. My first school, Central Primary, is now transformed to integrated education, a movement I have been proud to support from afar.

To childish minds in the Sixties we would have felt that Bangor spread its unique charms without favour but how better it is for us as adults to have learned to share – and hopefully protect – our unique and separate traditions.

Bangor is remembered in the Sixties as a blend of Englishness and Scots Irish, of genteel seaside resort, with a seasonal smattering of raucous, maybe obliging factory girl 'visitors'; of understated affluent 'residential villas' and discreetly situated council estates not impinging on the general ambience.

Strangely I feel more Irish now than I ever did when I lived in Bangor, but cocooned in its safe embrace in the Sixties gave a magical childhood at long last appreciated.

Members of The Power & The Glory pictured in March 1967 by the Ronald Graham Studio, Queen's Parade. From left: Deke Thompson (bass), James McCorriston (sax), Joe Hanratty (drums), David Montgomery (organ) and Pete 'Toot' Halpin (vocals). Inset is guitarist Harry Filmer, who missed the session.

1965

...the Spectator reports

INGLIS breadserver Ernest Thompson, of Bingham Street, retired in January after a career spanning 30 years. Having run his own milk round for six years, he joined Inglis in March 1934 and initially delivered bread to hundreds of local households by horse-drawn van. His last horse, Darkie, was in service for eight years. Mr Thompson had worked six 12-hour days a week.

Debra McDonald, of High Donaghadee Road, who had a piece of Christmas cake and a letter delivered to The Rolling Stones by *Spectator* reporter Jack Ledgerwood, received a letter from band member Bill Wyman, expressing thanks for the gifts. The letter was signed by the other band members.

Mick Jagger of The Rolling Stones is interviewed by *Spectator* reporter Jack Ledgerwood.
Spectator picture.

Bangor Rotarians paid tribute to former Prime Minister and wartime leader Sir Winston Churchill, who had died at the age of 90 on 24 January. Club president Hubert Nesbitt said Sir Winston's early life was already history, while his later life made him a national figure of the stature of Cicero or Abraham Lincoln. Past president David Magowan described him as the "greatest statesman the country has ever known."

"As he lies in state in Westminster, we think of those dark days of war and the comfort and courage he brought to us in those wonderful speeches over the radio," said Mr Magowan. "He gave us hope when all was darkness, and he made us laugh when there was precious little humour left in the world."

Derek Reynor (18), of 52 Churchill Park, was one of the Irish Guardsmen in the processional party at the State Funeral on 30 January.

Frank Russell with feathered friends in Ward Park. As an interesting aside, his Scottish-born grandson Derek Parlane (son of Frank's daughter Margaret) played soccer for Rangers from 1970 to 1980, followed by, amongst others, Leeds United and Manchester City. He was capped 12 times by Scotland.
Picture courtesy of Frank's granddaughter Fiona Collins.

Bangorians were saddened in March by the sudden death of Ward Park caretaker Frank Russell. Mr Russell, from Hamilton Road, was a familiar figure to the thousands who admired and fed the geese, ducks and other inhabitants of the park. A Belfastman, he had arrived in Bangor 45 years earlier, joining the Borough Council workforce in 1945.

The *Spectator* commented: "While Frank was in the park woe betide any dog not on a lead, or any cat which sought a rabbit for breakfast."His was succeeded as park caretaker by the appropriately named Billy Ward, who also lived on Hamilton Road.

Delegates from the North Down Imperial Unionist Association met in May to choose their candidate for the next Westminster election. The seven hopefuls included 44-year-old TV producer, writer and commentator Roy Bradford, along with sitting MP George Currie.

Mr Currie, who had represented North Down for 10 years, enjoyed newspaper headlines in advance of the selection meeting after he revealed that while a £30m Belfast shipyard contract to supply ships to the Indian Navy remained to be signed, he hoped this would happen within a week.

He subsequently secured an 18-vote majority over the combined total cast for the other six candidates, giving him victory at the first count. During the meeting he had read out a telegram from the London agents of the Indian company involved in the £30m order. "Pleased to report negotiations at advanced stage for shipyard order," it stated. "Firm announcement possibly within next 14 days. Will keep you fully advised."

A new bye-law in early May imposed an all-year one-way traffic system along Seacliff Road. Previously the one-way system had operated unconditionally during the summer months, but two-way traffic was permitted during the rest of the year between midnight and 10am. The Council sought the bye-law, which took effect from August 1966, because of the high number of accidents along the busy road.

The Bangor Laundry, one of the borough's oldest industries, was gutted by fire on the evening of 1 July. The building, between Hamilton Road and Broadway, was totally destroyed. Holidaymakers staying in the New Savoy Hotel had a particularly good vantage point because of its proximity to the laundry, which employed 40 staff.

By early July the cost of the proposed indoor swimming pool had risen to £227,000, with Council officers being instructed to negotiate a grant from the Ministry of Education.

The Rolling Stones before their Belfast concert appearance. Back (from left): Charlie Watts, Brian Jones, Bill Wyman. Front: Keith Richards and Mick Jagger.
Spectator picture.

At the end of July Bangor saw the last of the excursion trains that brought thousands of day trippers from Lisburn, Lurgan, Dublin and other areas each summer. This was because the direct link between the Great Northern and County Down Railway stations, on the outskirts of Belfast, was lost with the decision to demolish the Middlepath Street railway bridge to accommodate a new road. Fears that the Bangor to Belfast line could close on economic grounds proved unfounded.

Spectator reporter Ric Clark, who attended The Rolling Stones' concert at the ABC Cinema in Belfast on 4 September, wrote: "Off-stage the 'Stones' are a charming and dignified group of young men who are well educated and exceptionally clean. Each one is well-spoken and can easily engage in intelligent conversation."

On Wednesday 1 December two of Bangor town centre's oldest businesses were destroyed by fire – the drapery store of Messrs William Simon & Co. and the Singing Kettle Tea Rooms, which occupied two floors above Simon's. Damage was estimated at hundreds of thousands of pounds. But for the efforts of the fire crews, who managed to restrict the blaze to just one building, it could have been much more.

Bangor's two units were joined by appliances from Donaghadee and Newtownards, with 21 men and 10 jets being involved at the height of the blaze.

Christmas Shopping
WARNERS

THE COUNTY DOWN SPECTATOR
AND ULSTER STANDARD

BLAXNIT Pathfinder SOCKS

FIRE GUTS LOCAL BUSINESS PREMISES

Firemen's fine efforts saved other buildings

Records safe

WHY SHOP IN THE CITY THIS CHRISTMAS?

Anne Roulston

Mr. Reginald Maudling coming to Bangor

BADGES FOR BLOOD DONORS

Underwear Shop

Anne Roulston

ACCIDENTS

YOUR CHRISTMAS Gift Guide

Warner's

Firemen tackle the blaze that destroyed Simon's and the Singing Kettle. *Spectator* picture.

The alarm was raised by Ulster Transport Authority employee John Carlin, of Silverstream Park, a member of the overnight bus maintenance team at the Bangor depot. He saw the glow in the sky and called the police. During the resulting operation, cars were also removed from the adjoining showroom of Messrs H. &. J. McGimpsey.

The fire came at a very bad time for both businesses: Simon's was packed with Christmas stock and the Singing Kettle lost all its Christmas orders. Fifteen people were employed at Simon's; a number had worked there since leaving school.

George Kane, a director of Simon's, at the scene of the fire. *Spectator* picture.

The line-up for *The Palladium's Christmas Special*, broadcast on Ulster Television on Boxing Day evening, included Bangor-born magician Michael Allport, son of Mr and Mrs George Allport, along with Frankie Vaughan, Eddie Calvert and Jim Dale.

Sixty-five year-old James McKee, of 10 Belfast Road, retired on New Year's Eve after completing 52 years' service with the railways, having commenced with the Belfast and County Down Railway as a boy porter (earning 10/0d a week) and ending his career as an inspector. He served at every station between Bangor and Belfast, living through the steam era and its diesel engine successor. Mr McKee worked through both World Wars and recalled working "at all hours of the night" to help repair the lines after German bombing raids.

BANGOR MEMORY - The Bangor Link and Cadet Unit of the British Red Cross Society at their annual parents' night in May 1961. *Spectator* picture.

BANGOR MEMORY - Members of the Bangor Parish Youth Guild at a square dance in the Dufferin Minor Hall in January 1963. *Spectator* picture.

Rose Neill
...remembers

Rose Neill with parents Roger and Doreen.

RENOWNED as a one of our best known broadcasters and travel writers, Rose Neill was educated at Glenlola Collegiate, Bangor, until she was 11, The Mount School, York, and The City and East London College.

Her TV career began in 1977 as a presenter for educational programmes on Ulster Television. She also worked as a continuity announcer and newscaster for UTV and co-presented UTV's *Sportscast* with Jackie Fullerton.

She was headhunted by BBC Northern Ireland in 1985 to present the main news anchor programme *Inside Ulster*, its replacement BBC Newsline and other news bulletins and remained there for nearly 25 years.

MY Aunt Joan arrived at our house one very hot summer's day in 1965, when we children were playing in the paddling pool in the back garden with my mother.

"Can I take Rose out for a while, Doreen?" she asked. "Of course," said Mum. We were so hot and weary that the thought of a nice run in her car with the windows down sounded very enticing. I was the 'baby' and her wee favourite, so I suppose my siblings understood why they hadn't been included.

But without anyone knowing, she then took me up to the bathroom, washed my face and jammed me into one of my big sister Maxine's dresses.

The next thing I knew I was standing like a prune at

the edge of Pickie Pool with about 60 other little girls, a cardboard number emblazoned on my chest! It was the first ever Little Miss Northern Ireland competition. I got through to the top three and was promptly gathered up and taken home.

When my father Roger came home from the office that evening and heard what Joan had done he went MAD – nearly blew a gasket! "No daughter of mine will be in a beauty competition!"

But it was too late. I was then trailed along about two weeks later to the final, which I won, and the rest is history.

Auntie Joan wasn't too welcome at Raglan Road for a couple of weeks, until the steam died down, but we all laugh about it now!

Rose Neill – crowned Little Miss Northern Ireland in 1965.

She also presented a daily show on BBC Radio Ulster, three medical documentaries, various factual programmes, *Making a Difference*, and *Children In Need*. She is the longest standing newsreader in the UK, and for some time was the youngest newscaster too.

Her career with BBC Northern Ireland drew to a close in August 2008. Alongside a busy TV career and family life, for over 10 years Rose has been a travel writer, who has travelled extensively throughout the world reporting on the luxury end of the market.

Following her departure from the BBC she has moved back to UTV, presenting a documentary on the RMS *Titanic*, and now works as a newscaster and presenter.

Rose is an honorary patron of the Ulster Cancer Foundation and chairperson of the Riding for the Disabled Association.

Linda McAuley

...remembers

LINDA McAuley has been in broadcasting for 30 years, as consumer champion, documentary maker, and morning phone-in host. Cutting through red-tape and gobbledygook, Linda is best known for fronting BBC Radio Ulster's consumer affairs programme *On Your Behalf*.

However her career began in 1976 at Downtown Radio, the first commercial radio station in Northern Ireland, as a news reader and morning show presenter.

Her work was recognised in 2006 by the Trading Standards Institute. They voted *On Your Behalf* Best Consumer Programme, Radio and Television, and Linda was named Regional Consumer Journalist of the Year.

I SHOULD have been jumping for joy. We were on holidays, caravanning in Donegal and my father had just arrived with a very official looking letter addressed to me. It was from the Guide Headquarters, Buckingham Palace Road, London, telling me I had won first prize in the nine to eleven age group of the Girl Guides' 7th Art Competition for the Commonwealth!! And that my painting was going to hang there for a year. On top of that I would receive a beautiful box of watercolours from Windsor and Newton.

My parents were thrilled; Miss Mary Pyott-Shaw, who was my Brown Owl, and my friends in 2nd Bangor Brownie Pack were very impressed. The *Spectator* photographer even came and took my photograph! So why was I not enjoying the excitement?

Well you have to understand just how un-artistic I am to realise that winning an art competition was comparable to flying to the Moon – although that event had yet to happen!

Here's an illustration. When my youngest son, then aged six, was a member of the Beavers in Ballyholme, he told me that parents had been asked to come along and help them make Christmas cards. Would I come? I told him that of course I would, but that "I really wouldn't be much help."

He agreed! But as consolation he told me I was "very good at finding the end on the Sellotape!" And at the tender age of six he had summed up my artistic ability.

Pictured outside the McAuley family home at Ward Avenue in January 1968 followed the christening of sister Jan. From left: Carol and Linda McAuley, grandmother Jeanie Morrow and brother Simon.

But back to me as a Brownie. Every Tuesday I walked to the little wooden hut in Ward Park for Brownie Night. I was a "seconder" in the Fairy Pack and our uniforms were very different to those worn by Brownies today. A brown tunic and leather belt, a proper tie, yellow I think? And a brown beret. I still have my badge! And, of course, the badges we had won were stitched down our arms.

Linda McAuley today.

But how, at the age of nine, had I won a Commonwealth-wide art competition? Well I have to thank Brown Owl for her ingenuity. On that particular night we had been set the task of doing a painting and I had done my best – I think I'd painted my house with my Mum and Dad, brother Simon and dog Toby in the garden.

But just as I finished, with my usual clumsiness I knocked the jar of dirty painting water all over the table. Consternation all around, but Miss Pyott-Shaw came to the rescue and with a few tissues and a bit of black paint she turned the wet patch into an artistic cloud. I then forgot about the painting and the competition until my father arrived with that letter of congratulations.

I always felt I didn't deserved to win, and when, later

Linda and members of her family circle. Back row (from left): middle son Michael Andrews, sister Jan's husband Roger Beaumont and Linda's husband Paul Wilson. Middle row: Linda, brother Simon, mother Carol, father Tom and sister Jan. Front: Jan's children, Phoebe, Thomas and Ben.

that year, my Granny took me to London to see the painting hanging in this huge building next door to Buckingham Palace, I wondered if it was fair that my water accident had made me a winner.

I "flew" up to Guides, having won my wings a year or so later, and enjoyed Guiding as much as I did the Brownies. My three sons all benefited from being Cub Scouts, the youngest earning the Chief Scout Award. And I am proud to be a Guiding Ambassador. But I can't say I'm proud of winning that particular competition!

1966

...the Spectator reports

The Down County Health Committee agreed to develop a new clinic on the site of the former Territorial Army Centre in Castle Park (off the lower Newtownards Road). The plan was to bring all Bangor's doctors and surgeries together under one roof – along with the Health and Welfare divisions, then located at 44 Hamilton Road, and the clinic on Central Avenue. It was given the formal go-ahead in August 1968, at an estimated cost of £100,000, with work being completed in the early 1970s.

Addressing a meeting of the Dufferin Unionist branch on 21 March – nine days before the General Election – candidate George Currie explained why the Indian Navy order had failed to materialise. He said a Japanese firm had intervened with terms no British shipbuilder could match. With Roy Mason, then Minister at the Board of Trade, indicating special aid was no longer available, Mr Currie did not hold out much hope for the contract. However, he promised to bring pressure to bear on the Board of Trade.

Mr Currie was returned as MP for North Down, defeating Miss Sheelagh Murnaghan (Liberal) by 38,706 votes to 10,582 – a majority of 28,124.

Easter Monday, 12 April, witnessed 60 young members of the Northern

Youth campaign in Bangor

"Spectator" Photo

ABOUT 60 young people, members of the Northern Ireland Youth Campaign for Peace and Nuclear Disarmament spent Easter Tuesday afternoon in Bangor distributing leaflets and displaying posters calling for peace in Vietnam.

The group, led by 17-year-old chairman Terry Hooley, walked from Belfast to Holywood, then some hitched, some travelled by train and some walked to Bangor. They took up a stand at Queen's Parade and talked with passers-by.

"We are non-political," said Terry, "because politics in Northern Ireland is a dirty word." He added that they broke away from C.N.D. last August because of that organisation's politics.

Our photograph was taken at Queen's Parade.

Ireland Youth Campaign for Peace and Nuclear Disarmament visiting Bangor. They distributed leaflets and displayed posters calling for peace in Vietnam. The group was led by 17-year-old Terry Hooley, who declared: "We are non-political because politics in Northern Ireland is a dirty word."

With work on the Bangor ring road half completed, the second section, from the Newtownards Road to Clandeboye Road, was officially opened on 22 April.

In early July Bangor Borough Council turned down an application from Tonic Cinema owner Rank Odeon (NI) Ltd. for an extension to their cinematograph licence to allow them to show films on Sunday evenings during July and August. Councillors were equally determined to deny Bangor cinema-goers the chance to see *Fanny Hill* (an American version made in 1964), because it had not been granted a certificate by the British Board of Censors. Belfast City Council had agreed to it being screened with an A-Certificate, with the Councils in both Newtownards and Holywood adopting the same approach.

Pier fishing attracts enthusiasts of all ages during the holiday period. When this picture was taken last Friday several anglers had caught mackerel.
"Spectator" Photo

Councillors were warned in July that a storm from the north-east could completely sweep away the ageing wooden North Pier. Two alternatives were proposed – spending £30,000 to make the pier safe, or £11,000 to dismantle it. If it collapsed, they were told, the cost of clearing the harbour would be "substantially in excess of the cost of dismantling it now." The Council opted for the £30,000 scheme after receiving the promise of 50 per cent grant aid. Members were aware that, despite warning notices, the pier continued to be used by anglers who climbed over or around the safety barrier.

A 'Top Group' competition, held in August at Pickie Pool as part of the summer entertainment programme, was won by local band The Hoods, comprising Barry Woods (lead), Jim Crothers (bass), Eric Sterritt (rhythm), Pete 'Toot' Halpin (vocals) and Jim Dorman (drums). The runners-up were The Detours, who would rename themselves The High Wall in October. Band members were Harry Filmer (lead), Peter Mahood (bass), Trevor McCarroll (rhythm), Derek Drain (vocals), Michael Anderson (drums) and Alastair McKenzie (organ).

Also in August, ratepayers' representative Cllr Beryl Holland helped to form the Voice of Ulster's Christian Ladies. Its aim was to "establish better relations between all sections of the community, without the weakening or a sacrifice of our distinctive Protestant principles, but as a sincere endeavour for genuine neighbourliness."

Mrs Holland would lose her Ballyholme Council seat at the local government elections held on 17 May 1967. Two months after that the Ratepayers' Association folded, but the two events failed to deter Mrs Holland, whose letters in support of the Rev Ian Paisley became a regular feature in the *Spectator*.

It was announced in early October that a 40,000 sq. ft. extension to the Oneida Silversmiths factory on the Bloomfield Road held out the prospect of 200 new employees. It was hoped the total workforce would reach 600 by 1972.

The Aberfan Disaster of 21 October, in which 144 people, including 116 children, were killed after coal waste slid onto the Welsh village, touched the hearts of the nation, not least the pupils of Bloomfield Road Primary School. Being a new school it still lacked much equipment, which the children helped to purchase by donating 2d each per week. A portion of the school's savings, plus extra contributions, resulted in a donation of £14. 5s for the appeal fund. A separate appeal on behalf of the town raised £932. 3s. 5d.

Bangor man William Doggart, of Wellington Gardens – a member of the Newtownards-based family undertaking firm – was in charge of embalming operations at Aberfan.

In November Miss Maureen Fetherstonhaugh, a member of the Soroptimist Club of Bangor, made history when installed as the first president of the new Divisional Union of Soroptimist Clubs of Northern Ireland.

High Street businessman Arthur McFadden suspected the grimy painting left in to be cleaned in December might turn out to be an immensely valuable work by English landscape painter John Constable. The painting bore Constable's signature and was in his style, but Mr McFadden acknowledged this was not enough to prove it was genuine. And regrettably that proved to be the case.

Members of the P7 class for the school year 1965/66 at Connor House during a visit to the *Belfast Telegraph*. Included is headmaster Gordon Thomson.

BANGOR MEMORY - Barry's ice cream vans parked outside the children's funfair on the Central Pier in the mid-Sixties. *Spectator* picture.

Brian Wilson
...remembers

I SUPPOSE it is only with the benefit of hindsight that I can appreciate how fortunate I was to grow up in Bangor in the Sixties. It was an exciting time to be young and we enjoyed a freedom denied to our successors by the Troubles. We had just left the austere Fifties with its rationing and conformity to enter a new, vibrant and exciting decade of social revolution. However, as far as the Swinging Sixties were concerned they mostly seemed to pass me by.

In the Sixties the summers seemed long and hot and Bangor was buzzing with thousands of families from Scotland and the North of England, enjoying their Wakes Week beside the seaside. These tourists generated excitement as they flocked to Barry's Amusements, the arcades and to the concerts in the seafront hotels, particularly the Queen's Court, which regularly hosted top groups.

I recall in 1967 looking forward to a concert by a then unknown group called Procul Harum. I was surprised a few days later to watch *Top of the Pops* and to see the group perform its classic "A Whiter Shade of Pale." The Bangor date was cancelled and Procul Harum never did appear at the Queen's Court.

The tourists brought life and excitement to Bangor

NORTHERN Ireland's first Green Party Assembly member, lifelong Bangor resident Brian Wilson was born in 1943 and attended Trinity Primary School and Bangor Grammar School. In 1973 he left the Civil Service to do a full-time Masters degree in Politics at the University of Strathclyde.

He returned to Northern Ireland to take up a lecturing post in Omagh Technical College. In 1979 he transferred to Belfast's College of Business Studies as a lecturer in government and economics. For the next 25 years he worked as a lecturer / senior lecturer at BIFHE. Also in 1979 he married Anne (Cllr Anne Wilson) – they have two children, Scott and Allan, along with two children, Roy and Caroline, from Anne's previous marriage.

Since his Bangor Grammar School days Brian has had a keen interest in politics, with the aim of getting rid of injustice within Northern Ireland. In his late teens he joined the Northern Ireland Labour Party and campaigned for social reform. With the decline of the NILP he joined the Alliance Party in 1975 and over the next 20 years served the party in many different roles.

Elected to North Down Borough Council in 1981, he was Mayor in 1993/4, with Anne also holding the office a decade later. Brian left the Alliance Party in 1997, continuing his political service as an Independent, before joining the Green Party in 2004. He became the first Green Party representative to be elected to public office in Northern Ireland when again topping the poll in Bangor West. Success in the Assembly elections followed in 2007.

and provided a living for the owners of the hundreds of guesthouses and restaurants that surrounded the seafront. Unfortunately they disappeared in the early Seventies with the start of the Troubles and the arrival of cheap package tours to the sunny Mediterranean.

In the early Sixties I was a student at Bangor Grammar School and much more interested in sport than academic achievement. I remember being selected to represent Bangor on the BBC quiz *Sporting Chance* and reaching the semi-final. On returning from a victory over Hastings I was summoned to the headmaster's study. Instead of the anticipated congratulations, I was informed by Randall Clarke that I was wasting my time on the quiz when I should be concentrating on my A-Levels, due in two months' time. Of course he was right, but I would not have changed anything.

Bangor's *Sporting Chance* representatives (from left): Tom McVicar, Michael Rea and Brian Wilson. Back: Question master Brian Johnston, Cllr Jean Levine, chairman of Bangor Borough Council's Entertainments Committee, and scorer Roy Webber.
Spectator picture.

The long summer holidays provided wonderful opportunities to indulge in a great variety of sports. We usually played football or cricket at Connor Park, golf at Carnalea and during the Wimbledon fortnight tennis at Ward Park. However, despite living in "Ireland's leading seaside resort," I never had any inclination to learn to swim. This was no doubt influenced by my first swimming lesson at secondary school. On a freezing, windy April day we were lined up on the edge of Pickie Pool and ordered to jump in. I imagined I heard ice break and still shudder when I recall the impact of the cold water. This was my first and last lesson as I managed to avoid swimming throughout the rest of my school career.

My involvement in sport left little time for other interests although as a teenager I enjoyed fishing off the North Pier and messing about in Laird's Boats. Sunday afternoons were usually a time of rest and sitting on the wall at Queen's Parade, admiring the passing talent. Altogether it was a healthy out of doors life which I believe would benefit many young people today.

As the autumn drew in and the tourists departed, we began to focus more on indoor activities. The Tonic Teenage Show on Saturday mornings was a must, bringing a taste of the pop revolution that was sweeping Britain to Bangor. The hysteria created by the first playing of "She Loves You" helped me to understand the meaning of Beatlemania.

On Saturday evening the decision was which disco should we go to, the Duckpond or the Fo'c'sle, and in later years this became the choice between Caps and Milanos.

Starting employment as a civil servant reduced my sporting activities. The population of Bangor West was expanding rapidly and I became a leader in the new West Church Youth Guild. This contained a number of enthusiastic sportsmen and we started our own football, cricket and table tennis teams. The football team was pretty useless but we won the Bangor Youth cricket cup on two occasions and in our first year we won our section of the Bangor table tennis league.

I scraped into the team at number six, largely because I had a car and could take the team to away matches. Despite limited ability I enjoyed those matches, particularly the local derbies against St Gall's, when I normally battled against Edward Darling, later to become the Bishop of Limerick, or Roy Shephard, formerly of the *Spectator* and by then a feature writer with the *Belfast Telegraph*.

In addition to sport, my other lifelong interest is politics. This was a decade of political upheaval, highlighted by the American Civil Rights movement. Northern Ireland was not exempt and the events of the Sixties laid the seed for the conflict of the next 30 years.

I shared the optimism of many young people and supported the need for political change. I therefore backed the political reforms introduced by Prime Minister Terence O'Neill. I still believe if the people had backed O'Neill we would have avoided the 3,000 deaths we were to suffer during the next three decades.

I became involved in the campaign to "Keep O'Neill at the Wheel" and for many months I was involved in a heated debate with Beryl Holland, one of Mr Paisley's most ardent supporters, in the letters page of the *Spectator*. It is ironic that some 20 years later I worked closely with Beryl in the campaign to retain acute services at Bangor Hospital.

My most vivid memory of this period was the rally held by Mr Paisley outside St Gall's church to protest that the Catholic priest had been invited to a local meeting of residents of the rapidly expanding district to call for better bus services and leisure facilities for Bangor West. During his prayer Mr Paisley called on the Lord to destroy his hated enemy, the *Belfast Telegraph*. I said something inappropriate and was ejected over the hedge.

The decade which had begun with such excitement and idealism ended with frustration and a sign of the decades of violence that were to come.

1967

...the Spectator reports

Prime Minister Terence O'Neill visited Bangor on 14 January to lay the foundation stone for the new £400,000 Technical College in Castle Park. It was anticipated the College would be completed by Spring 1968, when its 2,300 pupils, then scattered in different buildings, would attend studies under one roof.

Milanos welcomed Dave Dee, Dozy, Beaky, Mick and Tich on 14 January. Other top artistes to appear there during the year included The Mindbenders, The Troggs, Del Shannon, The Small Faces and The Tremeloes. The rival Queen's Court Hotel enjoyed similar success in attracting big names that year, including Freddie and The Dreamers, Engelbert Humperdinck, Crispian St Peters and The Dubliners.

Headmaster Capt. Wilfred Hutton announced at the end of January that Garth House boys' preparatory school at Maxwell Road would close that July. The school, which catered for day pupils and boarders, had been founded 30 years earlier by Capt. R. G. Swanston. Capt. Hutton joined him as a partner two years later and succeeded him as principal in 1943. First based at Downshire Road, the school had moved to Maxwell Road in 1939.

Pupil numbers had fallen to just 20, and with closure impending, it was indicated they had all found places at other schools, including Rockport and Campbell College. Among its former pupils, who wore a distinctive red, gold and grey uniform, was Lord (Paddy) Ashdown.

Bangor suffered a major jobs blow in early February with news that the Heller confectionery factory on the Belfast Road would close in July. It manufactured Fox's Glacier Mints under licence and employed 48 men and 81 women. They fell victim to automation, with Fox's no longer needing to out-source production of their famous sweets.

Bangor Hospital Matron Susan Currie warned nurses in February against the practice of reducing their skirts to "mini" length. Miss Currie pointed out that some had their uniforms tucked up underneath their belts, which were so tight they could hardly breathe.
"If the girls think their uniforms are too long, they can come to me and I will get the seamstress to shorten them at the hem – not in the middle. We are members of a dignified profession, and we must be dignified in appearance," she declared.

The £150,000 Banks old people's home at Ballyholme was officially opened on 16 February by Lord Erskine, Governor of Northern Ireland. Accorded the honour of presenting flowers to Lady Erskine was the oldest resident, 94-year-old Miss Margaret Steenson, who had served as a nurse during both the Boer War and the First World War.

Sandie Shaw's "Puppet on a String," co-written by Derryman Phil Coulter (four years after appearing at the Tonic Teenage Show) and Scotsman Bill Martin, won the Eurovision Song Contest on 8 April. However, there was also glory for Bangor as the song placed second, "If I Could," was co-written by 35-year-old local man Wesley Burrowes. It was sung by Sean Dunphy, vocalist with the Hoedowners Showband.
Wesley's parents, Mr and Mrs Henry Burrowes, lived at Bingham Street, while his sister, Norma (22), a leading soprano and recording artiste of the future, was in her second year at the Royal College of Music.

NORMA BURROWES

Giovanni. The title role will be taken by Thomas Allen of the Welsh National Opera Company, Robert Lloyd of the Sadler's Wells Company

Army, Navy and Air Force personnel, along with members of the Fire Service, Civil Defence and Royal Ulster Constabulary, took part in a United Services Week in Bangor between 19 and 24 June. The event was launched in the Town Hall by Prime Minister Terence O'Neill who declared: "They have surely exploded at last the ridiculous idea that a whole generation should be judged by the antics of an idle fringe, who get all the

Members of the Trinity Primary School football team in the new strip purchased by the Parent-Teacher Association in April 1968. Back (from left): John Keenan, John Edge, Robert Foreman, Rodney Archer, Andrew Burke, Michael Goddard, Colin Canavan, Laurence Wilson. Front: Ian Wimpress, Garth Lewis, Roy Smyth, Michael Jacob and John Muir. *Spectator* picture.

publicity, yet represent only a tiny minority."

The Royal Navy flew in its carrier-borne strike bomber and all-weather aircraft and gave air-sea rescue demonstrations by Wessex helicopters, while HMS *Zulu*, moored in Bangor Bay, was open to the public. Royal Marines laid on a commando assault team, along with nightly demonstrations by the Red Arrows free-fall parachute team, while the RAF was represented by the Red Arrows aerobatic team. There were demonstrations of lifesaving and physical training by RUC, Civil Defence and Fire Service representatives.

A grand parade of all the services took place on the final day from the Luke's Point car park to Castle Park. It included an RUC contingent led by District Inspector Jack Hermon.

Garth House closed on 7 July, the final event being the annual pupils v. parents cricket match. Head boy Michael Quee presented gifts to Capt and Mrs Hutton and staff members, including Mr W. M. Maguire, Mrs Wanda Spencer, Miss M. Sheridan, Mrs Audrey Smith, along with Miss Eileen Swanston, daughter of the founder. Plans were subsequently submitted for bungalows and flats to replace the school.

Bangor-reared film producer William MacQuitty received an honorary Master of Arts degree at Queen's University, Belfast, in July. Mr MacQuitty had produced *A Night to Remember* (1958), which portrayed the sinking of the *Titanic*. He was also a key figure in the setting up of Ulster Television, serving as its first managing director.

Andy Johnston chaperones Little Miss Northern Ireland contestants at Pickie Pool.
Spectator picture.

The end-of-season prize distribution for members of Bangor Amateur Swimming Club, held on 21 September, also marked the retirement of Pickie Pool superintendent Andy Johnston after 46 years' service. He had given a countless number of children the confidence to take to the water for the first time. Three generations learned from "Uncle Andy," whose proudest boast was that in all his years there, there hadn't been a single accident. There was a standing ovation for Andy after he received a presentation from Cllr Jim Stark, who recalled how he had been saved from drowning by "Uncle Andy" back in 1927. Bangor native Mr Johnston, from 35 Ava Street, passed away, aged 71, on 13 September 1968.

It was announced in early October that work would begin within weeks on the third section of the Bangor ring road, from Bloomfield Road to the Groomsport Road. Councillors heard the contract would cost almost £500,000, but would attract a 90% Road Fund grant.

A Catholic clergyman took part for the first time in Bangor's Remembrance Day service, held on Sunday 12 November. The town's Royal British Legion had requested that all branches of the Christian Church be represented at the Ward Park Cenotaph; however, the decision on who participated had traditionally been taken by the Bangor Ministers' Fraternal, which comprised clergy from the Presbyterian, Church of Ireland and Methodist churches.

With the debate taking place behind closed doors, the ultimate decision to invite Fr P. J. McAtamney, Parish Priest at St Comgall's, to participate was taken in a personal capacity by Mayor Bertie Campbell. Fr McAtamney was unable to attend but was represented by Rev. Capt. Joseph Connolly (Church of the Most Holy Redeemer), who had been in Normandy for the D-Day Landings. Fr Connolly recited the exhortation: "They shall not grow old..."

The occasion also saw the unveiling of a plaque bearing the names of Bangor people who had been killed during the Second World War. Until then only the names of those killed during the First World War had been displayed on the Cenotaph.

Bangor FC manager Ralph McGuicken selected 16-year-old Billy Irwin to take the place of injured regular goalkeeper Alfie Wright in an Irish League match against Linfield on 19 November. It was Irwin's senior debut and although Linfield won 4-0, the youngster was praised for his efforts that prevented an even heavier defeat.

CAPPED AGAIN

Billy Irwin, the 17-year-old oalkeeper on the Northern eland team to play Wales in he British Youth International hampionship at Aberystwyth n Saturday, is a popular ounty Down youth, hailing om Donaghadee and playing

In Irwin's next two games Bangor were hammered 4-1 and 10-1, but having won County Antrim Shield and City Cup medals in 1969/70 and 1970/71, he was subsequently sold to Cardiff City, playing 180 games for the Welsh club between 1971 and 1978. He spent the remainder of his playing career in the USA. Irwin also gained two Northern Ireland caps at amateur level in 1971.

The *Spectator* of 15 December reported how the Bangor of the 1970s would be a major water sports centre if plans put to the Borough Council came to fruition. A yacht marina was suggested through the construction of a breakwater running from the North Pier towards Pickie Pool, while seafront developers could complement the scheme with new hotels, restaurants, shops, filling stations, etc.

Eileen Coates (née Walsh)

...remembers

EILEEN Coates (née Walsh) has lived in Ballyholme all her life. Until her retirement, she worked for Feherty Travel in the town. She and husband Derek have two daughters, Gillian and Helen, and they are now proud grandparents. Sister Lorraine lives in Killinchy. Married to Robert Dickson, the couple have two daughters, Jennifer and Catherine.

WHEN my father Harry Walsh was 18 he opened a shop on the Groomsport Road with a few sweetie jars and gradually built up his stock of confectionery to include groceries. He then opened a second shop next door specialising in hardware, tobacco and newspapers.

My father and mother Retta worked very hard in the Waverley Stores family business – up at 6am every day for the morning newspapers, arriving and organising the paperboys to deliver in the local area. Dad bought a Lambretta scooter and could be regularly seen delivering newspapers when a paperboy failed to turn up (usually when it was pouring with rain, or snowing!).

Over the years Dad employed many paperboys and one in particular, Raymond Parker (now managing director of Feherty Travel), became a lifelong friend and that friendship spanned over 40 years.

At around 6pm each evening a German Shepherd dog would bark loudly at the door of the shop. Dad knew just what to do. He folded the *Belfast Telegraph* in half lengthwise and put it into the mouth of the dog who took it to its owner in Waverley Drive. The owner said he never had to tell the dog to go to collect the paper; the dog just had an in-built sense to set off at that particular time every evening!

The two shops were open until 9pm, six days a week – a 15-hour day. The hardware shop was the only one of its kind in the Ballyholme area and you could buy a pound of nails, a box of screws or a few candles. There were no plastic bags to put the items in then – everything was either put in a paper bag or wrapped in brown paper and tied with string or sticky tape.

There were two windows in the hardware shop that we dressed on a fortnightly basis. I will always remember the way we got into one of them – there was a wooden partition at the back of the window with a little door opening into the window. We had to squeeze through this, clean the inside of the window with Windolene, be passed the items that were to be displayed, and then dress the window. It was a bit of a struggle to back out of the little door, whilst trying not to knock down any of the items on show – you had to be a bit of a contortionist!

There was an archway connecting the hardware shop with the grocery shop. One particular gentleman, who lived locally, always came in to buy his groceries on a Saturday afternoon and would only deal with Dad. He got his groceries 'on tick', i.e. the amount the customer owed was written in the 'tick book' every week and the customer settled his account on a monthly basis. I suppose it was the equivalent of our credit card system nowadays, but without the credit card!

Also my grandmother Elsie lived behind the grocery shop and one of the ways into her house via the shop was to squeeze round the back of the freezer and up a few steps into her living room!

Dad wore a taupe-coloured shop coat, just like Ronnie Barker's Arkwright in *Open all Hours* and the till was a drawer Dad had made, with a mousetrap set in the very back of it to hold the notes. This was a lethal piece of equipment – no Health and Safety worries in those days!

My sister Lorraine loved working in the shop on a

Shopkeeper Harry Walsh with young customer Natalie Andrews in 1971.

Eileen Coates and granddaughter Sophie.

Lorraine Dickson (née Walsh).

Harry Walsh's grandchildren (from left): Helen, Gillian, Jennifer and Catherine. Featured is the seat they purchased in his memory for the vicinity of the new Carnegie Library.

Saturday afternoon, but I hated it as I always seemed to get the customer who wanted a length of netting wire off a huge roll (which I was unable to cut), or a metal bucket, which I had no idea how to parcel!

Although our parents worked hard, with long hours, they enjoyed running the family business and many friendships were made with our very loyal customers. Mum and Dad ran the stores until their early sixties, when the business was sold.

Walsh's shop – the Waverley Stores – in 1962.

1968

...the Spectator reports

By early January Bangor Town Hall staff were preparing for the introduction of decimal currency in February 1971. Borough Accountant J. M. Devlin told the Council it would be necessary to convert or replace a number of cash machines used in various departments.

It was revealed in March that Bangor's ugly gasworks could make way for a dual-purpose conference hall and shopping centre, with a substantial car park to the rear. Alderman Charles Milligan predicted the future role of the soon-to-be-vacant site at a meeting of the Bangor Tourist Development Association.

Rank Odeon, owners of the Tonic Cinema, announced at the beginning of April they would be demolishing the derelict Connor House building in the cinema's grounds to enable them to redesign the car parking areas, providing better facilities and a firmer surface.

The derelict Connor House building in April 1968. *Spectator* picture.

Bangor's first traffic lights came into operation on Monday 8 April at the Belfast Road/ Abbey Street junction. Two more sets of lights were being installed, at Queen's Parade/ Bridge Street and at Warden's Corner (the junction of Main Street, Hamilton Road and Castle Street). The £11,000 project included pedestrian-operated "green man" crossings on High Street (near Quay Street) and in front of the Post Office at Main Street.

On Easter Monday, 15 April, Bangor Rugby Club won the Towns Cup for the first time since 1956. Captained by Bangor Grammar School teacher Matt Gillan, they defeated Dungannon 26-11 at Ravenhill. Other team members were: Conn McCall, Brian McClements, Ian Mencarelli, Denis Cooley, Brian Powell, Billy McConnell, Ross Jones, Rory Greer, Nicky Bailie, Harry Williams, Ray Moore, Hugh McCutcheon, Harry Edwards and Eddie Powell. Within days the club had added the Harden Cup and the Past Players Cup to the trophy cabinet. The Towns Cup was retained in 1969 and the club, with a new ground and clubhouse at Uprichard Park, was accorded senior status for the 1969/70 season.

Bangor man John Ringland, of 85 Skipperstone Road, returned home in May, six weeks after a life-saving kidney transplant operation at Addenbrooke's Hospital in Cambridge. The 41-year-old had suffered from a kidney complaint all his adult life and was kept alive by twice-weekly treatment from a kidney machine at Belfast City Hospital. Mr Ringland ended up with three kidneys – the new one and the original two, as the surgeon felt there was no need to remove them.

Kidney transplant patient John Ringland. *Spectator* picture.

The new flyover bridge and associated roads at the Belfast Road entrance to Bangor, linking the new dual carriageway to the ring road, was officially opened to traffic on 3 June.

Stock car racing arrived in Bangor that June as a new attraction for residents and holidaymakers. Staged at Bangor FC's Clandeboye Park, it involved Formula II racing, with at least 30 cars taking part each evening before crowds in excess of

3,000. Among the regulars was 22-year-old mechanic Adrian Lightbody, from Whitehill Pass, in his Ford Popular.

Summer graduates included William David Trimble, of 39 Clifton Road, Bangor. The former Bangor Grammar School pupil gained the degree of Bachelor of Laws with First Class Honours – he became the first QUB student in three years to achieve this. David Trimble, as he was better known, studied for his degree part-time while working in the Civil Service. Created Lord Trimble in June 2006, he served as MP for Upper Bann from 1980 to 2005, was leader of the Ulster Unionist Party from 1995 to 2005, joint recipient of the 1998 Nobel Peace Prize with John Hume, and inaugural First Minister of Northern Ireland in the newly-created Assembly.

Mr. DAVID TRIMBLE, who gained his LL.B. with first class honours

Many local students successful

Bangor Borough Council's vision of a seafront marina receded after members decided, in July 1968, to restrict the local authority to just the £30,000 scheme to improve the North Pier. Cllr Bill O'Hara commented: "Some day this marina is going to be built in Bangor. It would obviously be a lot cheaper if we started building it now, rather than waiting 20 to 25 years." The modern-day marina was officially opened in April 1989 – almost 21 years after this observation.

On 22 July eight-year-old Celia Hopkirk, of Farnham Park, Bangor, became the youngest person ever to swim from Pickie Pool to the North Pier. Accompanied by a member of Pickie's lifesaving team, she covered a distance equalling 13 lengths of the pool. She was the daughter of Mr and Mrs Frank Hopkirk and niece of leading rally driver Paddy Hopkirk.

Protesters who were demanding an indoor swimming pool for Bangor.
Spectator picture.

More than 1,000 placard-carrying children, accompanied by a large number of adults, marched to the Town Hall on 6 August to protest at the Council's failure to provide an indoor swimming pool. The demonstrators had formed up at Castle Street and then walked to the Town Hall via Main Street and Castle Park Avenue, arriving just before the Council's usual monthly meeting. A petition signed by 2,000 young people was handed over by Jim Thompson and Sandra McCann, from Bangor Amateur Swimming Club's lifesaving team.

Following a heated debate the Council adopted a recommendation to forward plans and bills of quantity to the Ministry of Education for formal approval. Furthermore, it was agreed that the Ministry be informed "the Council is anxious to proceed at the earliest possible moment" with the construction of an indoor heated swimming pool. The cost was estimated at just over £400,000, but Councillors believed it would be a pool "without equal in the country."

Multi-racial chart-toppers The Equals appeared at the Queen's Court Hotel on 19 August, prompting *Spectator* columnist Michael Wolsey to observe: "Real excitement has been missing from the local pop scene for a long time. It made a brief reappearance with The Equals."

Appearances by The Paper Dolls, supported by Bluesology (which Elton John had left the previous year), at the Queen's Court on 24 October, and Dave Dee, Dozy, Beaky, Mick and Tich at Milanos on 2 November, brought a lean year in musical terms to an end.

The new school year in September saw the opening of Grange Primary School. It was attended by 220 pupils from the Bangor West area under principal Hugh Boyd (29), who had been vice-principal of Bloomfield Road PS.

The creation of a Stormont constituency of Bangor, incorporating Bangor Borough, Groomsport and Ballygrainey, led to the new Ulster Unionist Party Constituency Association announcing it was seeking a candidate to contest the seat in the next General Election.

Reflecting the developing political crisis in Northern Ireland, Bangor Grammar School's Debating Society discussed the motion "That this house would emigrate from Ulster" on 11 October. For the motion, W. J. Martin said the Derry riots and Civil Rights marches showed people were "at last beginning to realise how sick our society is."

Dick Milliken, against, believed they were capable of recognising the weaknesses of their own Ulster society, "but if we emigrated, we could never hope to understand another society." He added: "All we need to do is adopt the same go-ahead methods of newer countries and we would not need to emigrate."

Brian Johnston, for the motion, feared there was "no hope for the thinking man in a society where one must be a Protestant or a Catholic, a Paisley or a Fitt supporter." He declared: "Anyone with ambition would emigrate from this corrupt society."

The motion was defeated by 13 to eight, with 27 abstentions.

Bangor Borough Council learned in November it could proceed with its plans for a swimming pool at Castle Park, beside the police station. The outcome of a meeting with Education Minister Captain William Long, it brought to an end a campaign dating back to the turn of the century.

"It was a wonderful morning," commented Mayor Bertie Campbell. "We all came away chirping like little dickey-birds. It was a wonderful relief to get this matter resolved."

Tenders were sought in early February 1969 and work on the two-year contract officially commenced on Monday 29 September that year.

Five candidates put their names forward for the new Bangor seat at Stormont, with all expressing their support, to varying degrees, for Prime Minister Terence O'Neill. They were: George Allport (56), a former member of Bangor Borough Council; Alex Beattie (35), a prominent Young Unionist; Hugh Bowman QC (46), who had no previous political experience; Bertie Campbell (55), Mayor of Bangor for the previous three years; and Harold Porter (48), a Comber-based member of North Down Rural District Council.

Following Terence O'Neill's "Ulster stands at the crossroads" broadcast in early December, the *Spectator* reported that Bangor man Frank Reid, of Abbey Drive, had ordered hundreds of car stickers bearing the slogan "Keep O'Neill at the wheel." These were available at the *Spectator* office, along with a petition supporting the Prime Minister.

The headmaster and 35 staff members at Bangor Grammar School wrote to the paper supporting Capt O'Neill's "policy of conciliation and reform." Their statement added: "We believe it is the only policy that will ensure our province will be a good and happy place for our pupils to live in as adults."

BROWNIE WEEK A BIG SUCCESS

THESE seventeen Brownies from 2nd Bangor Pack had a very enjoyable week together at Brownie House, Craigavad, from the 12th to 19th August. Front row (left to right)—Valerie Lyttle, Shirley McCaig, Lynda Strawbridge, Rosemary Ellison, Ann Cunningham, Adrienne McKee, Jane Woods, Joanne Drew. Middle row—Yvonne Heuston, Susan Stevenson, Deborah Feherty, Pamela Strawbridge, Rose Neill, Helen Baxter, Dawn Carter, Jill Driscoll, Valerie Chambers and guide Helen Feherty. Back—Pack Leader Donnie Parkinson, Brown Owl Mary E. P. Shaw, Cook Joy Connolly. The girls worked and played and sang together and, when rain kept them indoors, badges were worked for. Twenty-eight badges were gained in this way, and ten more swimmers' badges during an afternoon to Templemore Swimming Pool, Belfast, a highlight of the week's fun.

Photo: W. T. Kirk, Bangor.

Brownies from the 2nd Bangor Pack who spent a week at Brownie House, Craigavad, in August 1968. Back (from left): Pack Leader Donnie Parkinson, Brown Owl Mary Shaw and cook Joy Connolly. Middle row: Yvonne Heuston, Susan Stevenson, Deborah Feherty, Pamela Strawbridge, Rose Neill, Helen Baxter, Dawn Carter, Jill Driscoll, Valerie Chambers and Guide Helen Feherty. Front: Valerie Lyttle, Shirley McCaig, Lynda Strawbridge, Rosemary Ellison, Ann Cunningham, Adrienne McKee, Jane Woods and Joanne Drew.

Peter Millar
...remembers

PETER Millar went from Bangor Grammar School to Magdalen College, Oxford, where he studied French and Russian before joining the Reuters news agency in 1977. Following spells in London, Brussels, East Berlin, Warsaw and Moscow, he joined the *The Daily Telegraph* in 1985, subsequently moving to *The Sunday Telegraph* as Central Europe Correspondent. He moved to *The Sunday Times* in the same role in 1989, and was named Foreign Correspondent of the Year for his reporting on the fall of the Berlin Wall and revolutions in Eastern Europe.

He later became Deputy Editor of *The European*, working closely with Robert Maxwell which he describes as "like being aide-de-camp to Stalin." He is now a freelance writer for *The Times* and *The Sunday Times*, author of two novels, a travel book ('All Gone to Look for America', 2009), and a recently published memoir: '1989, The Berlin Wall – My Part in its Downfall' (Arcadia Books 2009)

PICKIE Pool. Castle Park. The shelters by the McKee Clock. Nowhere else much mattered if you were in your mid-teens in Bangor in the late 60s.

Winter was dead and dark and damp. We crawled to school before dawn, because the clocks had stopped going back – or forward – and watched the sun come up yawning in the back of Mr Bonar's history class. When the gales came lashing in off the Irish Sea and forked up High Street and Main Street, splattering ice-cold rain across the windows, my mother would tell me: "You wouldn't want to be down at the McKee Clock on a night like this." And I wouldn't. I still wouldn't.

In summer though, it was different. Life revolved around Pickie Pool. A freewheeling cycle ride down High Street, along Queen's Parade – on the wide pavement, eliciting 'tuts' from old ladies who dodged out of the way – to spend the day in skimpy swimming trunks, wondering if I dared to 'do the platty', a 12ft jump, nose gripped tightly, into murky green waters, and trying to ignore the showboats who dived – dived, Jesus, I ask you! – off the top board. I never even dared climb up there.

Or out the back, over the rocks and out to the raft, in the sea water itself – exactly the same as that in the pool,

Peter Millar today.

just a degree or two colder, having a slightly lower urine count. Then back in to sit on the wooden seats and sunbathe shivering beneath a towel looking up at the long legs of flat-chested girls in bikinis. And wondering when my time would come. Not at The Boulevard afterwards with 99s and giggles from the next compartment.

We wondered the same thing a lot too at night, in Castle Park, duffel coats pulled up, prototype hoodies, against the wind and rain – as we got older we even ventured out in winter – glugging from bottles of cider. Old English mostly, 3/4d a bottle, from the off-licence near the station ("You look 18, go on.") – cheaper than the Triple V that came in a bottle your mum might turn into a bedside lamp.

As a child the park had been a place to climb trees and invent fantasy worlds deep in the branches of an arboretum I thought was normal British woodland. As an adolescent it was a place to talk big and dream bigger. Depending on how much cider was consumed.

The McKee Clock shelters were an alternative venue. Sometimes you'd get the tougher kids there. Down from the Ponderosa. One of them put my head through a pane of the telephone box once. Nothing personal.

Pickie Pool.
Picture courtesy of the North Down Museum.

We discussed matters of global import: was it really Paul McCartney rather than Ringo Starr doing that funny little drum solo bit towards the end of the second side of *Abbey Road*. We carved our initials into the seats, now and then with a heart, and the initials of some girl from the Glenlola Fourth Form. I spent hours one languid sunny afternoon using my door key to carve two sets into the sandstone slabs that lined the sea wall along Queen's Parade. The fantasy of youth: engraving immortality in sandstone.

Judith Thurley

...remembers

BORN in Bangor Hospital, Judith Thurley attended school at Ballyholme Primary and Glenlola Collegiate. She took a degree in languages and later trained as a nurse at the Belfast City Hospital. Her first pamphlet of poems was published in 1995 by Lapwing Press, and her poetry has been published in Ireland, Canada and the USA.

She is co-author of two new books: 'A Natural History of Ulster' and 'A Wilder Vein.' She currently lives in Bangor and she teaches Maypole Dances to the schoolchildren of Holywood for their May Day fair. She is preparing her next full collection of poems for publication and editing an anthology of nature poetry.

HOW the memories come flooding back! To me, Ballyholme was the centre of the world, if not the universe. Growing up in Sheridan Drive, we could gauge on waking up each morning what the weather was like from the sound of the sea: nobody had heard of double glazing and our bedroom had sash windows which rattled if it was windy.

The sea was a living presence in my childhood. I understood from a very early age that the tide came in and out every six hours, but that high or low tide occurred an hour later each day and that Spring tides didn't only happen in Spring. In summer we were in and out of the sea all day, and we could run the hundred yards or so from front garden to beach in our swimsuits with beach towels flapping like capes.

I loved the thud of our bare heels on the pavement, and on very hot days the spots of melted tar on the soles of my feet, from crossing the Esplanade, were a kind of trophy awarded for exuberance and childhood daring. I had a secret ambition to toughen up my feet all summer so I would never have to wear shoes.

Judith (left) and sister Gillian on Ballyholme Beach.

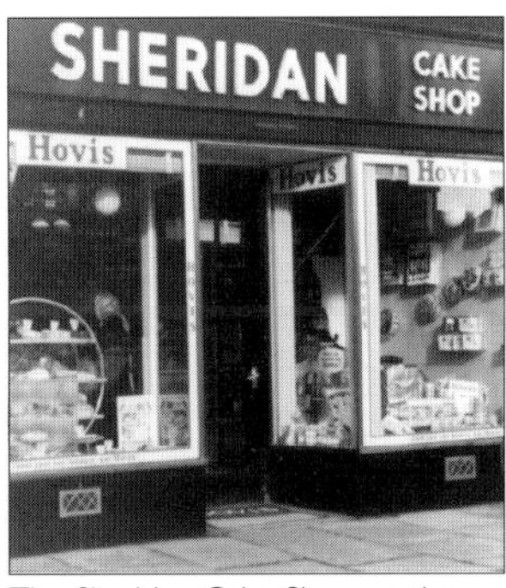

The Sheridan Cake Shop on the Groomsport Road.

We knew Ballyholme Bay intimately. Halfway between the tides, "on the way in," was best for jumping the waves and bathing, as the water was being warmed by the sand. When I was very little I actually believed we owned the steps at the top of Sheridan Drive down onto the beach. Our friends Lesley and Lorrie Walker, who lived in *Sealawn*, a B&B at 14 Ballyholme Esplanade, "owned" the steps at their end of the beach.

This seemed completely natural as each morning and afternoon we would rush home for lunch or dinner with the words: "See you at our steps or your steps?" We would then run home, past the chapel (which my brother mistakenly called the Church of the Holy Remember) and the house where the long-haired man with the Cork brogue lived with his friends with the van and electric guitars. We hadn't yet heard the word 'groovy', but we thought they looked 'dreamy' – our word for handsome and exotic. It was years later I learned this was Rory Gallagher and his band.

On Sundays we walked round the Point to Groomsport. In Spring we picked wild primroses from the tree-lined bank, which is now cut off by a fence that keeps the cows in and the walkers out. The primroses grew in such profusion there that their perfume drifted on the air.

I also remember peering through the hedge of the Dornans' back garden in Ashley Drive, where Sam and Eileen Dornan still live, and seeing the cows grazing in the fields that ran all the way to Donaghadee.

I remember all the shops: the Ballyholme Stores and the barber's, Richie McCartney's and the Sheridan Cake Shop, where we sniffed the aroma of freshly baked gravy rings on our way to school. There was Mrs Mills' butcher shop, McQuoid's grocery, which is lying empty now, and *While Away,* where we bought precious ornaments for Mum's birthday for 3d.

There was a strong sense of village community. In our street alone we had the McKees across the road and the Austins beside them. Grandpa Jack Austin was an old salt who kept lobster pots in the bay, and Penny, who I still think of as a little sister, and her mum Hazel lived there too, along with a mysterious old lady known only as 'the old aunt,' but I never saw her. Kind Mrs Duncan and the Jamiesons were on Lyle Road, and the O'Neills arrived at No 27 every summer to our delight.

On the other side of us were Pappy and Mrs Carroll, with whom we shared both back and front gardens, and the Martins lived beside Mrs Mills in an old rambling house that backed on to our street. They earned respect for having even more children than we had in our family, and for having a house full of animals, including Timmy the immortal cat, and a selection of rabbits, mice and stick insects. What good people they all were!

Judith Thurley today.

The Ballyholme Stores and Post Office on Sheridan Drive.

1969

...the Spectator reports

PLANS were announced in January by the Down County Education Committee to close Trinity Primary School from the end of June. The proposal – subsequently delayed to June 1970 because of difficulties in transferring the pupils to other schools – provoked an angry response from parents and staff. The decision was blamed on falling numbers due to the opening of several new schools in the area, particularly Grange PS at Bangor West. There had been a school at Brunswick Road/ Greenmount Avenue for more than 120 years, the longest period for any educational establishment in the town.

RADFORD IN THREE-CORNERED CONTEST

Alderman R. V. Campbell, the Official Unionist candidate, with his leading supporters. From left (front)—Mrs. Campbell, Mr. D. F. J. McAuley (chairman Bangor Unionist Association), Mr F. C. Tughan, O.B.E. Back — Mr. Robert Webb (election agent), Councillor Mrs Maisie McMullan (vice-chairman Bangor Unionist Association), Dr. M. Smyth (chairman Clifton Unionists), Mr. A. Beattie, Councillor J. Preston (chairman Dufferin Unionists), Mr. H. Bowman, Q.C.

Independent Councillor Bertie McConnell dropped a political bombshell by declaring his intention to stand in February's Stormont election – as a Progressive Unionist supporting the Prime Minister. Meanwhile, the five Unionist candidates set out their stalls at a selection meeting, with Mayor Bertie Campbell emerging victorious. With 236 delegates from seven branches attending, he achieved 150 votes on the second ballot, with Hugh Bowman his closest rival. Mr Bowman proposed the selection should be unanimous, a call seconded by George Allport and agreed without dissent.

Successful candidate Bertie McConnell with jubilant supporters. Included are Mr and Mrs Hubert Nesbitt, Noel Ince, Michael Pyper, Horace Hamilton, Mr and Mrs Bill O'Hara and Mrs McConnell.
Spectator picture.

Mr McConnell, who had represented the Clifton Ward for 11 years, romped home to become Bangor's first MP with a vote tally that surprised even his own supporters. The constituency had 20,000 voters and there was a 61.87 per cent turnout. Mr McConnell received 7,714 votes, compared to the 5,190 cast for sole opponent Bertie Campbell.

Election agent Hubert Nesbitt declared that the margin of victory "surpassed our highest expectations." Mr McConnell attributed his success to a "great groundswell of liberal opinion in Bangor" and said he intended to seek the Unionist whip at Stormont. He was offered the whip by Capt. O'Neill and accepted it. Mr McConnell's success was, in fact, one of the first manifestations of what would become the Alliance Party – formed in Mr Nesbitt's Waverley Drive home in April 1970.

It was the end of an era when the Tonic closed for major refurbishments on 10 March. Three weeks later, and following expenditure totalling £50,000, the cinema reopened as the Odeon Theatre, sharing its name with every other picture house owned by the UK-wide chain. The public, while appreciating the plush new seats and carpeting, did not like the name and within a few years the Tonic identity was restored.

The victorious Bangor Grammar School rugby team with the Schools Cup. *Spectator* picture.

Bangor Grammar School won rugby's Schools Cup for the first time in its history, beating 18-times winner Campbell College 6-3 at Ravenhill on St Patrick's Day. They had previously reached the semi-finals in 1938 and 1939, when the captain was Hugh Greer, later a popular bookseller in the town. Three decades on the captain was Dick Milliken, one of nine players who had won the Medallion Shield three years earlier. Eighteen thousand cheering fans of both sides watched a pulsating final, settled by Robert Forsythe's second half penalty kick. The other points were secured through a try by Billy

The crowd cheers on Bangor Grammar (above), while it's a tense moment on the bench for coaches Jimmy Welsh and Matt Gillan, along with vice-principal Bertie Styles (below). *Spectator* pictures.

Bangor supporters at the Schools Cup final (from left): Valerie Sandys, Roz Elwis, Marion Wilson and Joan Carter.
Spectator picture.

Kirk. The team's joint coaches were teachers Jimmy Welsh and Matt Gillan.

International acts were thin on the ground in 1969, with the first of the year being a return visit by Dave Dee, Dozy, Beaky, Mick and Tich to Milanos on St Patrick's Day. This was followed by Roy Orbison on Easter Monday (7 April) and The Move on 17 May, both at

Milanos, Dave Berry at the Queen's Court Hotel on 18 September, and, finally, Tiny Tim at Milanos on 8 November.

The *Spectator* reported on 21 March that former West Belfast MP James Kilfedder was considering a bid for the Unionist nomination to fight the North Down seat at Westminster in the next General Election. The London-based barrister had lost his West Belfast seat to Gerry Fitt (Republican Labour) in March 1966.

Kilcooley Primary School, named after the large estate that provided most of its pupils, opened on 15 April. The initial enrolment was 170, but the school had room for 700 pupils – the number anticipated would arrive over the course of the following year. The school had been build for £180,000 to relieve pressure on other primaries in Bangor West.

Michael Wolsey, writing in his new *World of Wolsey* column on 25 April, reflected on the growing crisis in Northern Ireland: "... and now British troops are on guard here, how long will it be before they extend their job to that of policing the country? How long before the British Government takes over completely. I do not think either move would be particularly good, but at the moment I see little alternative.

"I do not believe we are on the verge of civil war, but I do believe it is only a matter of time before we see the first death in a riot. Shots were fired by a policeman in Derry. I don't blame the man; he had good reason to panic and he did, apparently, fire in the air. But, nevertheless, a gun has been used. Murder seems only a step away. Can the British Government bear this on its conscience? I pray not, for I doubt if our own government has one."

George Best and other members of the Northern Ireland team travelled with manager Billy Bingham to Bangor on 9 May, to visit the Special Care Centre on the Ballyholme Road. The team bus later went to the seafront, where some players enjoyed putting on the small green close to the McKee Clock while others shopped. George Best did neither – he got pinned against a wall at the foot of High Street and spent almost half-an-hour signing autographs for eager fans.

Bangor Art Club realised the long-cherished dream of having its own clubroom. At the annual general meeting, held in the art room of Bangor Technical College on 30 May, members learned the club had acquired the former Girl Guide clubroom close to the Carnegie Library.

Work started in June on a £600,000 shopping centre at Springhill, on the outskirts of the town. The plans envisaged a large food store, a furniture showroom and at least 20 different shops, along with a bank, restaurant, coffee lounge and crèche, plus a petrol station and parking spaces for 800 cars. The developers hoped it would attract 10,000 customers a day.

The BBC's *It's A Knockout* came to Bangor on Saturday 7 June, although the home town side, captained by John Oettinger, had been defeated at the qualifying stage the week before, leaving Coleraine and Fermanagh to do battle in Castle Park for a place in the European *Jeux Sans Frontières*. Some 4,000 spectators watched an assortment of games, most involving water, including one where two team members had to walk along swaying planks with containers of water wedged tightly between their foreheads. With presenters David Vine and Eddie Waring and referee Arthur Ellis on hand, the show was broadcast on BBC1 the following Wednesday. Coleraine emerged victorious, but the BBC's policy at the time of reusing video tape to save money means the programme no longer exists.

THE MAD WORLD OF THE "KNOCKOUT" AT CASTLE PARK

"IT'S A MAD mad mad mad world." At least that's what it looked like at Castle Park last Saturday at the Northern Ireland heat of "It's a Knockout" which was broadcast on B.B.C. television on Wednesday evening.

CECIL'S SECOND SINGLE

THE FABULOUS ADVENTURES OF MARCO POLO

WASHABLE SKIRTS
THE LONG AND THE SHORT OF IT!
100 HIGH ST SMYLIE BANGOR

CLOUD No 9 BANGOR
TWO TOP GROUPS
FRIDAY CIRCLE | SATURDAY GUMM

A White Paper issued on 2 July proposed that Bangor and Holywood should be administered by a single authority. It envisaged an area stretching from Groomsport to Craigavad and Ballyhackamore, combining Bangor Borough Council and Holywood Urban Council with parts of North Down Rural Council and Castlereagh Rural Council. The White Paper proposed 16 new Councils for Northern Ireland; in fact 26 were created with the reorganisation of local government in 1973.

Fifteen-year-old Bill Wolsey, of 65 Church Avenue, flew to London in early July for a trial with Terry Neill's Arsenal. A pupil at Bangor Technical College, he had played most of his soccer for the school side. Bill also took part in the Irish Schoolboys trials in 1968.

The *Spectator* of 15 August reported that two local policemen had been injured during rioting in Londonderry. In addition, many refugees from the violence in

Belfast had arrived in Bangor to stay with friends and relatives.

Prime Minister James Chichester-Clark, who had succeeded Terence O'Neill on 1 May, called on all members of the Ulster Special Constabulary to report for duty to their nearest police station. Rioting had spread throughout Northern Ireland but North Down escaped the violence. One minor incident involved slogans being daubed on a side wall of St Comgall's RC Church on the Brunswick Road but they were quickly removed.

A month-long ban on all parades meant the Royal Black Institution demonstration scheduled for Bangor in late August did not take place. The ban was subsequently extended and even applied to Remembrance Day parades, with Bangor ex-Servicemen gathering in the Earl Haig Hall on Hamilton Road that November.

Rodney Bambrick and fellow organist Miss Ethel Miskelly, who arranged for the organ to be stored in a barn near the Primacy.
Spectator picture.

The Tonic name wasn't the only casualty of the Odeon Theatre changes, the *Spectator* reported on 26 September. Another was its famous Compton organ, whose glass-covered console used to rise from the orchestra pit.

After the owners decided to put it up for sale the organ was purchased by local teacher and musician Rodney Bambrick, who wanted to install it in the town's proposed new county secondary school.

At a meeting in the Queen's Hall, Newtownards, on 15 October, James Kilfedder was selected from 11 contenders to represent the Ulster Unionist Party in North Down at the next Westminster election. Sitting MP George Currie had been eliminated on the first ballot after receiving fewer than five per cent of the votes. Some delegates openly referred to the episode of the Indian Navy contract that never materialised in 1965.

Mr Kilfedder would go on to win the 1970 General Election with almost 70% of the votes. He represented the constituency at Westminster as an Ulster Unionist, an Independent Unionist and an Ulster Popular Unionist until his death in March 1995.

With the violence persisting, a ban was placed on the sale, use or discharge of fireworks at Hallowe'en 1969. In a related measure, Bangor was chosen as the first police station from which RUC members would go out on duty without firearms. In addition, British troops from the Royal Hampshire Regiment were billeted in Bangor hotels and guesthouses for a 48-hour break after being in the midst of six weeks of intense street rioting in Belfast.

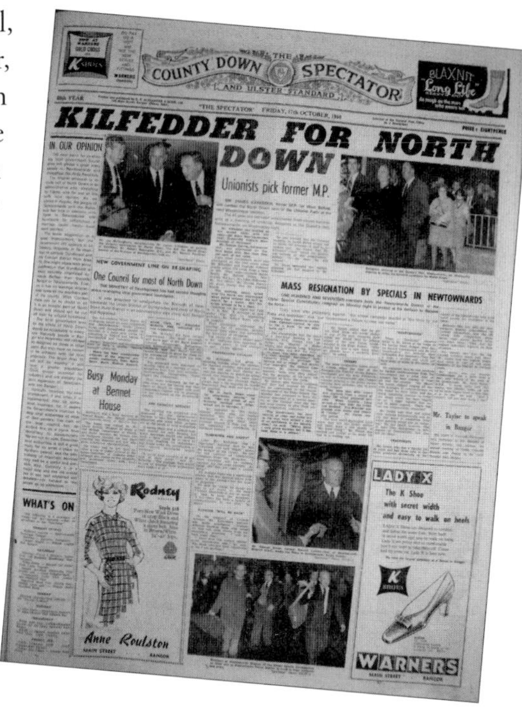

THE COUNTY DOWN SPECTATOR AND ULSTER STANDARD

KILFEDDER FOR NORTH DOWN

Unionists pick former M.P.

IN OUR OPINION

NEW GOVERNMENT LINE ON RE-SHAPING

One Council for most of North Down

MASS RESIGNATION BY SPECIALS IN NEWTOWNARDS

Busy Monday at Bennet House

Mr. Taylor to speak in Bangor

WHAT'S ON

Joe McCaugherty congratulates Jim Kilfedder on gaining the Unionist nomination in North Down for the next Westminster election. The MP for North Down at Stormont, Robert Babington QC, and Dennis Faulkner, brother of Minister of Development Brian Faulkner, look on.
Spectator picture.

A 2-2 draw against neighbours Ards on 18 October put Bangor FC into the final of the City Cup – their first senior final since the 1962/63 season when they were beaten by Linfield in the Co Antrim Shield. Glentoran thrashed Bangor 7-1 at Windsor Park 10 days later, the consolation goal being scored by Tommy Craig.

Northern Ireland captain and Arsenal centre-half Terry Neill was married to London model Sandra Lichfield in First Bangor Presbyterian Church on Tuesday 4 November. Bestman was the groom's brother-in-law Terence Doak. Friends and relations – but no stars from the two teams – were entertained to a champagne reception at the Crawfordsburn Inn and the couple honeymooned briefly in Paris. Terry was back in London by the weekend for a First Division match against Brian Clough's recently promoted Derby County. Arsenal won 4-0.

The bells of St Comgall's Parish Church rang out on Wednesday night 26 November to mark the appointment of the rector, Archdeacon George A. Quin, as Bishop of Down and Connor in succession to the Rt. Rev. Dr Frederick Mitchell.

The year, and the decade, ended on a depressing note for local teenagers with the enforced closure of their only dance venue, Cloud 9, which was held on Saturday nights in the Co-Operative Hall at Market Lane. Bangor Borough Council ordered its closure following critical remarks by Resident Magistrate Albert Walmsley at a juvenile court in Holywood.

The case before Mr Walmsley had involved drugs and led to a 13-year-old girl being placed "under the care and protection of the court." The Cloud 9 teenage dance was mentioned in the evidence and this, coupled with earlier complaints about under-age drinking, resulted in the Council ordering the Belfast Co-Operative Society to terminate its contract with the dance's organisers.

Two hundred young people signed a petition protesting at the closure, but to no avail. Cloud 9, which had lasted two years, was the first teenage club to feature lights and music, along with mirrors, projectors and "all the paraphernalia that goes to make a psychedelic dream," commented Michael Wolsey in the *Spectator.*

Roisín Mc Donough
...remembers

ROISÍN Mc Donough has been Chief Executive of the Arts Council of Northern Ireland since 2000, working in central and local government as well as in the community and voluntary sector throughout her career. She was involved in the Opsahl Commission in 1992, established to find a way forward to resolve the then political impasse in Northern Ireland.

Currently she is a trustee of the Creative and Cultural Skills UK Board and chairs the Northern Ireland Women Chief Executives' Forum. She's been a lifelong Hispanophile, a passion developed whilst at Glenlola Collegiate.

I ARRIVED in Bangor in the late summer of '65, returning to my birth town, after an interlude of 12 years, from Nairobi, Kenya, where my father had worked helping to train the Kenyan Air Force, post Uhuru or independence. Kenyatta was in power, the Mau-Mau problem temporarily at bay and my parents' nomadic existence had come to an abrupt end, symbolised by the eventual arrival at my maternal grandparents' home of the standard issue RAF crates, which contained our family's few possessions.

So this was where our new permanent life was to be; in a small, northern Irish provincial seaside town painted from a sombre palette of muted greys and browns; a place characterised by a white-faced uniformity and a life lived in-doors: or so it seemed.

This was a whole different world of sounds, smells and colours to which I would have to adjust, once again.

A few weeks later, at almost 15 years of age and, secretly sporting my beaded elephant hair bracelet under my new school uniform (later remembered by friends as being terribly exotic), I stepped into Form 4 at Glenlola Collegiate, over-awed in my repeat status as an "outsider."

When I left in 1970 to head to Trinity College, Dublin, it was a very different Bangor than the one to which I had returned five years previously. Inevitably I, too, was a different person, partly due to the passage of time, but more because of the profound experiences, friendships and events that shaped me during those formative years.

My Bangor eventually ceased being alien, at least for a brief while. Superior teenage seafront sniggering at the sandwich board religious zealots; under "The Clock" not-so-secret assignations; self-made clothes cut out from sewing patterns and material bought in the Spinning Mill; hysterical shrieks as our sadistic sports teacher pushed us into the heart-stopping cold sea water at Pickie Pool every Tuesday; furtive gulps of cheap vodka and lime (more often than not spat out!) in the toilets at the train station before a night out at the dance at the Duckpond hall – all of this gave way to lazy, long nights, usually in the summer, spent on Crawfordsburn beach or at sleep-overs where intense friendships were formed amidst the wreckage of passionate discussions about life, war, love, politics, poverty, injustice, protest and civil rights.

We argued over whether it was right to send men to the Moon when so many were dying from starvation in Biafra; we denounced French colonialism through the pages of Albert Camus; we revered Simone de Beauvoir's refusal to accept anything less than being seen as equal to her lifelong companion and lover, Sartre; we quoted e e cummings to each other and the Russian poet Yevtushenko gave meaning to Marx's Communist Manifesto.

We listened intently to Simon and Garfunkel, The Rolling Stones, Jimi Hendrix but our real heroes were Bob Dylan and our own Van the man Morrison. We occupied the school playground in a sit-down protest against "authority - man" and my friend Cherrie and I travelled to Paris in search of Baudelaire's version of revolution – at least in our heads, I think that was it.

And, as our own unfolding descent into Northern

Ireland's version of horror took place, we also struggled to understand that and what it meant for us. Bangor, an overwhelmingly protestant town and a reasonably affluent haven in North Down, far from being immune, was expanding and struggling to cope with the overspill of sectarian strife from Belfast.

People living in the area stopped talking to us, ever so politely, in the run-up to the Twelfth; my parents counselled against certain places frequented by squaddies; I was reminded that I was only one of two catholic girls in a protestant grammar school and, as a family, we watched with dismay how the Civil Rights marchers were attacked.

A cautiousness had descended and Bangor, my Bangor, not only had altered, it had started to shrink in terms of its possibilities.

Roisín Mc Donough (back, second left) with members of the Glenlola Collegiate netball team who beat Newtownards Technical College in the 1969 County Down League final to go through to the Northern Ireland championships. Also included (back): Sandra Johnston, Judith Page (captain), Maureen McNally. Front: Olive Kent, Chris Head and Jeanette Baxter. *Spectator* picture.

Bangor's music scene in the 1960s

Trevor Hodgett
...an introduction

BORN and bred in Bangor, Trevor Hodgett, who attended Bangor Grammar School in the Sixties, is the co-author, with Colin Harper, of *Irish Folk, Trad & Blues: A Secret History* (The Collins Press). He is the jazz and blues critic of *The Irish News* and has contributed to *Mojo, NME, Sounds, Record Collector, Jazzwise, Blues In Britain, Folk Roots* and other publications, to reference works such as the *Guinness Rockopedia*, The *Mojo Collection* and *The Encyclopaedia of Music in Ireland*, and to BBC, Downtown and RTE radio and television programmes.

THE Sixties didn't arrive in Northern Ireland until the Eighties, local wags are fond of joking. Or indeed the Nineties or even the Noughties, depending on who is making with the wisecrack.

It's an amusingly self-deprecating idea. But it isn't true. Or, at least, it's not true as far as Bangor is concerned. Sure, there may have been backwaters in Northern Ireland where the kids were grooving to the outdated sounds of Big Tom and the Mainliners and Wee Mick and the Hootenannies. But in Bangor, notwithstanding the town's image as a bland, suburban nowheresville, a youthful, bohemian sub-culture thrived.

So it was that almost contemporaneously with hipsters in London listening to mid-Sixties blues bands like The Rolling Stones and The Pretty Things in funky clubs like the Marquee and the Flamingo, hipsters in Bangor were listening to blues bands like The Hoods and Blues Unlimited in funky clubs like the Red Rooster and the Crypt.

And, a year or two later, almost contemporaneously with hipsters in San Francisco listening to bands like The Grateful Dead and Country Joe and the Fish in psychedelic clubs like the Fillmore, hipsters in Bangor

The Hoods, from Bangor, winners of the top group competition at Pickie in 1966. Standing: Jim Crothers, Barry Woods (with umbrella), Eric Sterritt. Seated: vocalist Pete 'Toot' Halpin and Jim Dorman.
Spectator picture.

were listening to bands like Taste and The High Wall in psychedelic clubs like Cloud 9 and the Electric Honey Pot.

Of course, commercial chart bands were popular in Bangor as they were everywhere else and the hitmaking likes of The Kinks, The Small Faces and Roy Orbison regularly drew large crowds of girls – and large crowds of boys who were drawn to the large crowds of girls – to the Milanos ballroom on the Seacliff Road.

And just across Kingsland from Milanos, past the pitch and putt course and tennis courts, musically conservative showbands like The Dave Glover Band

TASTE IN HONEYPOT

THE TASTE, from Cork, generally rated as Ireland's number one pop group, have fallen on good times.

The trio has just arrived back in Ireland after a highly successful tour of London's top clubs. They have now made London their base and will soon be returning there before starting on a tour of England and Scotland.

They have also signed a recording contract with a major record company.

The Taste will be playing a few dates while back home, one of which is in Bangor. This Friday they will top the bill at the Electric Honeypot.

and Dickie Rock and The Miami were entrenched in Caproni's, where the eccentric, old-school manager is reputed to have ritually ironed every banknote before paying the night's performer.

Sneering at the local ballrooms with their outdated strict dress codes, heavy bouncers and commercial music policies, the local bohemians, however, were instead captivated by the cutting edge musical culture of the time.

From 1963, for example, the sort of electrifying, highly sexual, amped-up blues played by the Stones and the righteously angry, idealistic and poetic protest music of Bob Dylan and Joan Baez were being fanatically followed by the town's cognoscenti.

Hordes of alienated, denim-clad teenagers would drift through the streets at weekends, hanging out in the amusement arcades, sharing alternative ideas, playing guitars and generally grooving on the idea that they could and one day would make the screwed-up world a better place.

Bands proliferated, comprising enthusiastic hopefuls besotted with the music and with the idea of having an alternative lifestyle, of avoiding the nine-to-five commuter grind that they witnessed their stressed-out dads grimly enduring.

In truth, for most such escape was a fantasy. The High Wall's pianist Ali McKenzie did become a pop star in Suzi Quatro's band, and guitarist Rory Gallagher, a Bangor resident, became a blues legend – and a victim of the bluesman's lifestyle. But most ended up donning the suits they dreaded, becoming teachers or civil servants or estate agents just like their dads.

Or, in the case of The Power & The Glory and Blues Unlimited organist David Montgomery, becoming the Editor of the *News Of The World* and the chief

The Detours, beaten finalists at Pickie Pool in 1966. From left: Trevor McCarroll, Michael Anderson, Derek Drain, Alastair McKenzie and Peter Mahood. *Spectator* picture.

executive of Mirror Group Newspapers.

No frills clubs like the Fo'c'sle and the Duckpond provided outlets for local blues bands, and gathering places for like-minded fanatics to debate the relative merits of Muddy Waters and Howlin' Wolf, of John Lee Hooker and Lightnin' Hopkins.

And then the scene evolved. Blues began to seem prosaic as the world turned technicoloured and the psychedelic revolution transformed rock and popular culture. The Beatles evolved from cute parent-endorsed moptops into parent-alarming acid heads intrepidly exploring previously unimaginable musical territories, The Grateful Dead and others introduced instrumental virtuosity and extended, mind-expanding jamming into rock – and Bangor teenagers were as quick as any in the Western world in latching on to the thrilling new developments.

New clubs emerged to satisfy the needs of Bangor's turned-on teenagers such as the Electric Honey Pot, Cloud 9 and the Magic Roundabout, the names suggesting the drug culture that was by then central to Bangor's music scene.

"Teenagers of the Borough unite, you've nothing to lose but your chains," declaimed one advert in the *Spectator* for the Magic Roundabout, suggesting the radical fervour and mischievous wit of the times. Hilariously the ad went on to denounce the "capitalist reaction from the right wing Bangor oligarchic faction," by which they meant the grey-suited straights of the Borough Council.

Equally evoking the spirit of the times, an advert for the Electric Honey Pot advised readers to "TUNE IN – DROP IN – FREAK OUT – LIVE AND LOVE" and promised "FLOWERPOWER FOR EVERYONE."

In a photograph taken by their father Dick, Trevor Hodgett and his brother Richard are seen with their mother Sheilagh.

Bands like Rory Gallagher's Taste were regulars in Bangor's hippie clubs along with visitors from the English counterculture such as The Crazy World of Arthur Brown, remembered nationally for their extraordinary hit *Fire* and remembered in Bangor for the way in which Brown freaked out the stoned teenagers in the audience by setting fire to his hair as part of his hallucinatory stage show.

But somehow Bangor's bohemian heyday waned. LSD use remained common into the Seventies and dope smoking became endemic but other, stupider drugs, like the sedative Mandrax, gained popularity. The motive was less often to achieve a higher state of consciousness. The motive now was to get smashed, to get totally off one's face, and Bangor Hospital found itself busy at weekends pumping out the stomachs of those who were self-destructively pursuing oblivion.

Trevor and his wife Trish Keogh-Hodgett.

By and by the hip clubs closed and so did the ballrooms and Bangor became a desert for live music. In the town nowadays young people get their kicks dancing to records in nightclubs and no doubt, as young people ever will, they have fabulous fun.

But old-timers reflecting on the Sixties will perhaps feel they were the generation who lived through the best of times, that they were the ones who had the thrill of believing they could change the world, that they were the ones who had a sense of optimism and of new possibilities that was truly intoxicating.

Such idealism foundered on the rock of the Troubles and in the face of the horrors that were unleashed no subsequent generation has been able to believe, as Bangor's hippies once naively and sweetly did, that human beings have the innate goodness to create an idyllic world. That surely is a loss.

**Seaside Rock* (North Down Museum, 2003) by Colin Harper and veteran Bangor scenester Sam Gibson were helpful in writing this article.

Mason Douglas
...remembers

Spectator picture.

SON of Mr and Mrs Victor Douglas, of Ava Street, and one of a large family circle, Mason settled initially in Vancouver after emigrating to Canada in 1968 then, after a spell in Toronto, where he worked for the local school board doing maintenance work and glazing, he moved to the rural area of Hardwood Ridge, New Brunswick.

During his time in Toronto he had maintained his interest in music and, as a member of a locally-based band, supported both The Kinks and The Fortunes. For a time he was joined by two former Bangor men, Ray Caulfield (Clandeboye Place), on rhythm guitar, and John Gavin (Clandeboye Road), on drums.

Following the move to New Brunswick he hadn't sung for some 30 years until the late 1990s, when he was coaxed to sing again at charity and benefit concerts. These days he prefers Country and Western songs and Irish ballads, along with a little bit of light rock 'n' roll.

MY early musical experiences in Bangor came as a member of the town's Salvation Army junior band. I also liked Slim Whitman and Hank Snow, but everything changed for my generation when Elvis Presley arrived on the scene. His singing and his whole style just swept me away. After that you would rarely have found me without a mouth organ and the bones [for percussion].

The first band I ever sang with was called Margo and The Hepcats and they were based in Donaghadee. Indeed, the first time I was ever on stage as a singer was with the band in Donaghadee Orange Hall. However, my big break came as a 17-year-old, in April 1962, when I wrote to Ulster Television's musical director Tommy James in the hope of getting a spot on the evening magazine programme *Roundabout* [which later evolved into *Teatime with Tommy*]. Along with more than 30 other hopefuls, I went along for an audition and sang some of my favourites by Elvis, Karl Denver and Buddy Holly. Tommy must have liked my voice because I was able to sing "That's All Right, Mama" on the show later that month.

Not long after that I met up with the other members of The Janitors, who'd come together about a year

Mason Douglas (left) during the early 1970s in Canada with Bangor men Ray Caulfield (centre) and John Gavin.

earlier while most of them were still at school. We'd sing and play together on the sea wall at Queen's Parade on Friday and Saturday nights, but then the Tonic Teenage Show started and we seized our chance.

We were promoted as the big local band when it opened in January 1963, but we didn't actually play too many shows at the beginning. We would go along out of curiosity if there was a band from Belfast playing so we could check out the opposition. But then we heard about their *Way To The Stars* talent competition and, of course, we had to enter it.

At the beginning of our performance I wouldn't go on the stage. Instead, the other band members would open with The Tornados' "Telstar," which was note perfect and sounded just like the record. Then the curtains would open and I'd make my entrance, wearing a sealskin dinner jacket, microphone in hand

Mason Douglas near his home in New Brunswick, Canada. Picture courtesy of Sandra Hennessey, Minto, NB.

and acting like I owned the place. I'd be singing the Ray Charles classic "Tell me What I Say" and the girls would just start screaming the place down.

It was a really fun time and it didn't matter that the prize we received for actually winning the group section in the competition was just £5. Nor did it lead us to the stardom we'd hoped for. There were no big talent scouts at the Tonic Teenage Show, just the weekly reports in the *County Down Spectator*, which, if nothing else, helped to make us big names in our own town.

After The Janitors I joined The Seasons Showband, with an appearance at the ABC/ Ritz in Belfast high among my memories. At the time I was working in the Gasworks because my older brother Vincent already worked there, but I always hoped for a career as a professional singer. That chance came in July 1966, by which time I was working as a glazier with S. Miller (Bangor) Ltd., of upper Main Street. I quit my job there and joined The Idaho Showband as a professional singer. I really hoped it would be the big one and we certainly had some fantastic times but in the end I decided to emigrate to Canada, in 1968, and I've been here ever since.

Like so many of my generation I don't feel my age. I have very fond memories of those wonderful days on the stage in Bangor and it's very flattering to hear people say that bands like The Janitors inspired them to pursue their own career in music.

Tonic Teenage Show artistes

Raymond Grant did a comedy act
at the Tonic Teenage Show.
Spectator picture.

Victor 'Chunky' Douglas.
Spectator picture.

The Saints, featuring Victor 'Chunky' Douglas.
Spectator picture.

Tonic Teenage Show artistes

The Meazzie Showband from Belfast, featuring 19-year-old Marilyn McWhirter from Abbey Park, Bangor. *Spectator* picture.

The greatest band that never was! This publicity picture from 1963 for the Tonic Teenage Show features musicians and friends (from left): Peter Baird (organ), Jim Gregg (drums), Nevin Robinson (guitar), Colin Barnes (vocals) and Billy McClintock (bass). *Spectator* picture.

Anne and Jack Chambers.
Spectator picture.

Belfast band The Vaqueros.
Spectator picture.

Deke Thompson
...remembers

DEREK 'Deke' Thompson moved from Belfast to Bangor at the age of 11 and attended Bangor Grammar School until 1963. During the Sixties he played bass guitar in The Janitors, The Dimensions, The Power & The Glory, The John Smith Band, Fagan, and The Bangor Folk Four. In the early Seventies he joined the road crew of Chips, who were playing on the Irish Showband circuit, before working as an audio-visual technician until the early Eighties.

Deke then began a career in film and television as a sound recordist and remains so to this day. He has filmed in Africa, America, Asia, Australia and Europe on a wide range of programmes and films, ranging from the Ulster Orchestra through acoustic folk music to rock 'n' roll, commercials, short films and documentaries.

EVERY time I go to a gig I am amazed at the quality of the sound created by the musicians on stage and the audio engineer at the back, mixing his sound sources and sending them to the amplifiers and speakers on or above the stage, but it was not always as good as this. Back in the Sixties sound equipment, and the resulting quality, was far removed from today's audio highs.

I used to say that at the start of the Sixties you could walk along the street with your guitar in one hand and your amp in the other. By the end of the decade it would take two people to comfortably carry the amplifier.

My first amplifier was 10 watts (providing a similar sound output to most TVs), with one five-inch speaker. The controls were very basic, with volume, bass and treble tone controls. That was it.

When I joined The Janitors, we realised that our small amplifiers would not be usable, so after looking around the Belfast music shops we bought a Selmer Selectortone amplifier with two 12-inch speakers and a 30 watt power section. This was a revelation – two channels each with two inputs with

An early version of The Janitors pictured in December 1962 to mark the launch the following month of the Tonic Teenage Show. From left: Alistair McKendrick, Mason Douglas, Mike Cash, Terry Higgins, Deke Thompson, Nevin Robinson and Richard Morrow. Included is Mrs Dorothy Higgins who initially handled the record requests.
Spectator picture.

channel one having a reverb unit. It's hard to imagine that all four guitar players connected to this at one of our first gigs, Rock at the Ranch in Helen's Bay, which used to feature traditional jazz. After one or two weeks we just had to buy another amplifier designed for bass use – a Selmer Bassmaster, again 30 watts with two 12-inch speakers.

Vocals were a different matter. As we had only one singer, Mason Douglas, we hired a microphone, a 35 watt Phillips PA amplifier, and one column speaker cabinet which had about six five-inch speakers.

Playing at the Tonic Teenage Show, we found a Phillips PA amplifier but with a 140 watt output feeding a 15-inch speaker at either side of the stage and, again, only one microphone. When it came to the final of the *Way To The Stars* talent competition in 1963, we placed the microphone just behind the speaker of Terry Higgins' keyboard. The sound of the keyboard filled the theatre as we played "Telstar."

Deke Thompson today.

Compare that to today's bands with eight or so microphones just round the drum kit, microphones on each instrument and on each amplifier in the back line, tens of thousands of watts in the PA system, and thousands of watts for the monitors on stage so that the band can hear vocals and other instruments.

Other amplifiers came and went during the decade. Selmer faded but Vox were always there, especially after The Beatles chose them, but then came Marshall – separate amplifiers and speaker cabinets became the most wanted items. Other manufacturers, including Orange, HiWatt, Carlsbro, etc., joined the fray. PA systems developed with "Crazy Boxes" and their Lisburn copies "E Boxes", with six 10-inch speakers in each, becoming the PA for most bands.

It was not until the mid-Seventies that PA systems began to develop into what we know today.

Members of The Power & The Glory at Ward Park in Bangor. From left: Deke Thompson, Harry Filmer, David Montgomery, James McCorriston, Pete 'Toot' Halpin and Joe Hanratty.

Richard Morrow
...remembers

Spectator picture.

THE thought of heading out for an evening of cabaret entertainment in the then very popular Half Door Club, at the rear of the Royal Hotel, and to be served a plate of bacon, eggs, potato bread and ketchup, seems nothing short of a self-inflicted early death in this day and age.

I was fronting popular group The Carpetbaggers at the time, and we were under the personal management of the late great James Young. We were in London one week when we received a telegram (as only James would have done) to tell us he'd secured a six-week cabaret season at the venue owned and run by Bill and Anne O'Hara.

This was music to our ears. James came down the next Sunday afternoon and transformed our American-imported way out sounds to *his* suggested cabaret sounds, including numbers like "Oh My, Papa," "Scarlet Ribbons," some Irish numbers, and even a Spanish song.

Just what the public *here* wanted and indeed it worked and opened our music to a wider audience. Well done Jimmy!

On the bill was Marie Cunningham with Irish tenor Peter Tomelty. The comedy was in the form of Sidney Dodsworth and George Carroll, who formed that great mime act The Recordites. Indeed, these days George is

RICHARD Morrow arrived on the local entertainment scene as a 15-year-old Bangor Grammar School student in 1961. Joined by Christopher Duffy (14), lead guitar, Michael Cash (17), rhythm guitar, and Alistair McKendrick (16), drums, he was vocalist and bass guitarist with his first band, The Janitors. By 1963 and still at school, he was a regular fixture as DJ with Colin Barnes at the Tonic Teenage Show.

Further DJ work followed at the Plaza Ballroom in Belfast, supporting Brian Rossi and the Golden Eagles. Richard later returned to the band scene with The Carpetbaggers, who toured extensively, released several well-received records and supported many big names of the day. They were the only Northern Ireland band in the Sixties to be billed with The Rolling Stones.

In subsequent years he combined his musical talents with his business

Members of the Carpetbaggers and friends during an early Sixties visit to see Santa at Robbs in Belfast. Included are Roy Slinger, Tom Corran, Mike Swanston, Colin Sanderson, Richard Morrow, Andy McAvoy, Alistair Stewart and Colin Barnes. Picture courtesy of Colin Barnes.

still music assistant with my Hypnosis Show.

I recall we went on stage at 9pm as the last pieces of the greasy fry were being demolished by somewhat under-the-weather patrons (as the bars closed at 10pm!). We had to enter the area through the kitchens and every evening Bangor's well known barber Sammy Graham was in charge of the stove!

Those were the innocent days of fun, music, happiness, and a simple night out when we were all home by 10.30pm. It was a time when the only drugs we knew were used in hospitals, when we drove if we could see with *one* eye, and we filled the tank of the car for a fiver.

They were days when, if you knew the owner of the hotel or bar, you might get that late drink at 10.20pm!

Those were the days my friends, we thought they'd never end. But they did - although there are plans for a Carpetbaggers reunion!

acumen to create, produce and promote many different stage events. For the past two decades Richard has enjoyed a very successful career as a stage hypnotist, combining his unique comedy style with his refined skills to tap into the realms of the inner mind. He has performed at venues around the world and is a very popular entertainer on cruise liners.

Still based in his native Bangor, he has also assisted numerous people to stop smoking through hypnosis.

Internationally renowned stage hypnotist Richard Morrow.

The Carpetbaggers in February 1967. From left: Richard Morrow, Alistair Stewart, John McAuley, Norman Fusco and Paul Lyttle. *Spectator* picture.

Alastair McKenzie

...remembers

Spectator picture.

ALTHOUGH it may have seemed like any other New Year's Eve, 1959/60 was a pivotal time for the Baby-Boomers of the late Forties. Our ages were, at last, in double figures and we eagerly awaited becoming teenagers.

The austerity years, filled with food rationing and Perry Como, were ending, with bland safe family entertainment giving way to the hedonistic excitement of Rock'n'Roll; the new youth culture of The Beatles and The Rolling Stones.

In an earlier life... Scouts of the Fox Patrol (1st Bangor Troop) and the Wolf Patrol (3rd Bangor Troop) who finished second and third respectively in the 1963 County Down Scout Challenge Flag competition. Wolf Patrol (back, from left): Patrick Taylor (leader), George Lowden, Tom Bleakley, Dick Milliken, Simon Yaul, Peter Phillips. Fox Patrol (front, from left): Tony Bell, James Moore, Neal McCay (leader), Bill McCready, Alastair McKenzie and Roger Gough.
Spectator picture.

FORTIES – Born Glasgow, move to Bangor.
Fifties – Ballyholme Primary School. Piano lessons (Robert's Cup at Bangor Music Festival).
Sixties – Bangor Grammar School and Queen's University. The Detours, The High Wall, The John Smith Band. Move to London.
Seventies and Eighties – Various club and pub bands, Suzi Quatro Band (several No1 singles and albums worldwide), Slack Alice, Lonestar.
Nineties and Noughties – Return to Bangor. Red Hot Roosters, duo with Lawrence Thompson, Purple-Headed Blues Band, Blues House, The Flange Band...

The cover of Suzi Quatro's self-titled debut album in 1974. From left: Dave Neill, Alastair McKenzie, Suzi Quatro and Len Tuckey. Below: Alastair McKenzie in the Seventies.

Queen's Parade in Bangor during the summer was a mass of day-trippers, visitors, bars and amusement arcades. It still had a sandy beach and a long sea wall, which stretched from the McKee Clock to Pickie Pool. There you could sit and watch an endless stream of humanity on warm sunny weekend evenings or even watch the coal boats unloading on the Central Pier.

At home, radio listening changed to telly watching; but radio fought back with dedicated music stations like Radio Luxembourg, while the stuffy and formal Light Programme on the BBC gave way to Radio One – after a bit of encouragement from the pirate Radio Caroline.

This was the time of Telstar, Yuri Gagarin and the Vietnam War. Transistor radios were changing technology, and it was essential to have a record player to play the new 7" 45rpm and 12" 33rpm plastic discs that, amazingly, would not break if you dropped them.

Youth organisations did their fundraising by having Saturday Nite Discos, which also started to include live bands and that particularly appealed to me. Fifth Bangor Scouts had their long-established Fo'c'sle and First Bangor Scouts started their 'Saturday Nite at the Duckpond' in Ward Park, just down from the hospital. The Crypt at the Ward Park bowling green pavilion saw in New Year 64/65 with Van Morrison, Billy Harrison and Them and strengthened my resolve to play in a live band.

Milanos on Seacliff Road was a proper dance hall, built on the ruins of an old cinema, which brought us the delights of The Small Faces, The Kinks, and, most notably, John Mayall's Bluesbreakers, featuring Mick Taylor, who shortly afterwards joined The Rolling Stones.

The Queen's Court Hotel on Queen's Parade had live music most nights of the week, with special acts like The Equals with Eddie Grant, and Dave Dee, Dozy, etc. Just like Pickie Pool, it had its talent competitions, which saw my band The High Wall do pretty well against stiff opposition from an amazing young guitarist called Gary Moore, who astounded everyone with his virtuosity at the tender age of 13.

The Co-op Hall, off Market Lane, brought us established Belfast bands and then the Electric Honey Pot at the British Legion Hall on Hamilton Road trumped the lot with the best live band ever. Few could ever forget The Crazy World of Arthur Brown – keyboards, drums and singer Arthur, coupled with a brilliant light show and fiery theatrical props, ably supported by the ubiquitous High Wall, of course!

Alastair McKenzie with popular roadie Philip Barr, a veteran of the Sixties music scene. Picture courtesy of John Miskelly Photography.

Taste arrived in Bangor from Cork shortly afterwards, featuring the fabulous Rory Gallagher, who

Still making music today – Alastair McKenzie (right) with members of the Bangor-based Flange Band. From left: Nathan Simpson, John Hodge, Seonaid Murray, Roger Davidson, John Caulfield, Aaron Campbell and Brendan McGreevy.
Picture courtesy of John Miskelly Photography.

held court every night of the week at their house in Sheridan Drive at Ballyholme. Try and keep us away! What a star, but a delightfully unassuming chap.

Towards the end of the decade of love-ins and psychedelic happenings, youthful exuberance, optimism and over-indulgence, the clouds started to gather, and events would occur that resulted in many young people leaving Bangor to seek their fortune elsewhere. Some would never return.

James McCorriston
...remembers

Spectator picture.

ALTHOUGH Newtownards born and bred, James McCorriston earns his place in "Bangor in the Sixties" through his involvement with The Power & The Glory, one of the town's leading bands of the era.

He subsequently played in three Belfast bands (one of them out of Queen's University). In 1971 he headed for Canada in a band formed for that express purpose. After the group broke up and a year (1973) in Hollywood, California, playing in a band there, James finally settled in the Toronto area in 1975. He was in three more bands until 1978, when he ended up a "one man band" and made a living as a solo artist for the next 20 years.

After being a professional musician for 30 years he has now been out of the business for the past decade, during which time he has worked for the local gas utility. He says he felt the time was right to hang up the saxes and guitars.

I WAS in two local Ards groups before the Bangor-based The Power & The Glory, the second of which came out of Regent House (the Newtownards equivalent of Bangor Grammar School). That would have been from 1963 through to 1966, playing a mixture of pop and R&B.

The Power & The Glory came together out of an interest the six of us had in American "soul" music and the songs of Otis Redding, Wilson Pickett, Sam and Dave, James Brown, Tamla Motown, and UK bands such as The Vagabonds and the Big Roll Band. We were strictly soul, which is one reason why the name just seemed to fit. It was David Montgomery's suggestion. He was reading the Graham Greene novel of the same name at the time and proposed it to us at a band practice early in the game. The fact is, we all loved it.

Besides playing locally, our favourite gig was probably the Stella Club in Dublin, as we returned there many times to a great reception.

During the short life of the band (1967/68) our main competition locally would have been Haggy (Alastair) McKenzie's group The High Wall. In fact, after our demise, our drummer Joe Hanratty joined

James McCorriston during a visit to Belfast's Crown Bar in 2008.

them. For all the rivalry it was common for members of both bands (and future Chips singer Paul Lyttle) to be found sitting in a group on the sea wall at Queen`s Parade just shooting the breeze. They were halcyon days indeed!

One thing unique to the P&G (in my own musical career) was that when we first started off, we would run Friday or Saturday dances on those weekends we weren`t already booked. It was a way to generate a little cash and to give us something to do. Sometimes we`d play ourselves, but often as not we`d hire one of the Belfast bands to come down for the night.

Once in a while it would be a "double bill" if we had enough "trusties" to mind the box office, etc. Bands such as The Styx (not the later version!), The Few and Just 5 all performed. We called the club the Magic Roundabout, which predated Cloud 9 and the Electric Honey Pot (ah yes, psychedelia!).

That legendary soul man Sam Mahood, the vocalist of Just 5, had already achieved a certain notoriety on the music scene, although I thought his singing voice was questionable to say the least. However, as a character he was very popular and beloved by all. It fell to me, and my non-musical buddies, to do the posters for the dances at the Magic Roundabout and so I got it in my head that Just 5`s first gig there should be billed as "Sam Mahood and Just 4".

Well, when the band hit Bangor, they also hit the roof. They were furious, threatening not to go on stage, and had to be placated. Except that is for Sam who was all smiles and obviously appreciated the personal recognition. I had to do some fast talking to get out of that one!

Another incident I clearly remember was a gig we played at the Electric Honey Pot (the British Legion Hall on the Hamilton Road). We'd hired a young local group as the "warm up" act and were relaxing in the dressing room waiting for the designated time to go on stage, when suddenly organist David Montgomery burst into the room in a state of agitation.

"Right lads, they`re repeating," he said, indicating that the young group had exhausted their repertoire and had begun over again. I guess he thought we should bail them out and go on ahead of schedule. All he got was a few withering stares and looks of disinterest from the rest of us. What he didn`t know was that those four fateful words would be echoed numerous times, to tease him, in the months that followed!

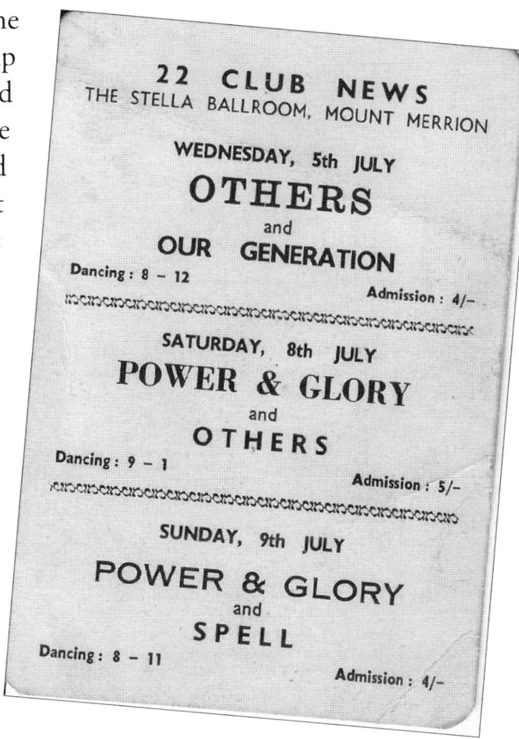

An advertising leaflet from the summer of 1967 for the Stella Club in Dublin.

Outside of Bangor

Geoffrey Bowman
...remembers

THE older and smarter brother of the compiler of this book, Geoffrey was born two days late, at Bangor Hospital, on Saturday 13 November 1954, and has maintained that standard of punctuality ever since. Lacking the qualifications to become an astronaut, he settled for the legal profession and now specialises in asbestos litigation as a partner in the leading Belfast firm of solicitors C & H Jefferson.

Geoffrey's closest experience to space flight was as a solo glider pilot during his student days, soaring silently over Scrabo Tower and generating four times normal gravity while performing high-speed aerobatic manoeuvres. In all, Geoffrey has made 286 glider flights, only one of which involved an unplanned vertical landing on a Newtownards barbed-wire fence.

His fascination with all things space-related has taken him to Kennedy Space Center twice to witness manned launches and he

IT is rather important to bear in mind that for those of us who were growing up in Bangor in 'The Sixties,' there was no sense of a clearly defined decade in the way that we now think of it. The summers were warm and sunny, the winters were cold and snowy, and from one year to the next, between Monday and Friday, 39 weeks a year, we went to school.

I didn't really appreciate The Beatles or The Rolling Stones in their heyday: that came later, helped by an element of nostalgia. But if popular music was one thread running through the fabric of what would be called 'The Swinging Sixties,' another thread defined the decade in a way that history will remember long after the more ephemeral memories of popular culture. The Sixties was the decade of the Space Race, and it culminated in the first human footprints on another world.

It was the launch of Yuri Gagarin on 12 April 1961, which fired my enthusiasm for all things to do with space. My father helped me to cut out pictures of the first spaceman from the local papers and to paste them into a scrapbook. Three weeks later we did it again when America blasted Alan Shepard into space. I still have those pictures, and I really wish I'd kept my

Geoffrey Bowman surrounded by memorabilia from July 1969, when man walked on the Moon for the first time.

has met 10 of the 12 Apollo Moonwalkers. (When he met Neil Armstrong in 2003, they chatted about their shared interest in gliding.)

In recent years Geoffrey has gained much enjoyment travelling to some of the world's more remote destinations, including Easter Island, Greenland, Spitsbergen, Alaska, the Yukon, the Falkland Islands and Tierra del Fuego. He keeps threatening to write about his experiences "because there just aren't enough travel books out there."

To date his published work consists of several magazine articles about aviation and space flight, but in Spring 2010, the Nebraska University Press will be publishing 'Footprints in the Dust' about the Apollo missions, to which Geoffrey has contributed two chapters. He says his wife Sandra can't contain her excitement.

father's newspaper from a summer morning in 1964, when a picture of the Moon, taken by an American spacecraft, was splashed across the whole of the front page. (Come to think of it, the kamikaze probe was splashed across the surface of the Moon!)

The Russians made the first space-walk and were first to launch a three-man spacecraft, but by 1968 their challenge was faltering and the voices I heard transmitting Christmas greetings from lunar orbit were American.

In Spring 1969, Dad booked our summer holidays and I was horrified to discover we would be away when the first attempt to land men on the Moon would take place. With some persuasion from me, he eventually agreed to change the arrangements, but this meant travelling home on 20 July, the day of the landing.

A *Spectator* cartoon from July 1969, suggesting the Moon's 'residents' did not welcome the American astronauts!

Geoffrey Bowman with Neil Armstrong, first man to walk on the Moon. Picture courtesy of Darragh Henry.

After a number of delays and misadventures we made it back to the house with barely half-an-hour to spare and I rushed into the living room to switch on our venerable black-and-white TV.

The crackling voices from space came through loud and clear and when the lunar module touched down in a cloud of dust I carefully wrote down Neil Armstrong's historic words: "Tranquillity Base here, the *Eagle* has landed." I still have that scribbled note.

Geoffrey Bowman with Buzz Aldrin, second man to walk on the Moon.

Almost seven hours later we were again assembled in front of the TV watching those eerie grey images of Armstrong as he stepped onto the surface of the Moon and uttered the defining quotation of the decade, the century and the millennium: "That's one small step for a man; one giant leap for mankind."

In answer to the question, "Where were you when man landed on the Moon?" I can record that the Bowman family were in our own living room in 22 Waverley Drive, Bangor, County Down, Northern Ireland, Planet Earth.

Gilbert Nesbitt
...remembers

BORN in 1951, Gilbert Nesbitt lived briefly in Glenburn Park, then from the age of two to eight at 4 Waverley Drive and thereafter to adulthood at 20 Waverley Drive. Queen's University Law Faculty, September 1969 to June 1973 (LL.B); Ohio University, January 1974 to 1976 (MA); trainee solicitor, 1976 to 1978; solicitor 1978 to the present day with Wilson Nesbitt, Solicitors.

I WAS a sickly child. Bronchitis kept me off primary school a lot of the time. I think in my first year, at nursery school, I totalled only a handful of intermittent weeks for the whole year. Life was spent lying in bed reading Enid Blyton and playing games like draughts, ludo, Sorry and snakes and ladders with any passing victim, particularly my poor Gran who quickly learnt I had to win – punctuated with the odd unusual event such as the dentist or the barber appearing instead of the doctor.

I got extra coaching in English at home for the 11-Plus from a Mr. Glenn who must have done a reasonable job because to my surprise I achieved just enough marks to get a marginal pass and move to the next stage (a tactic I would continue to later perfect). So off I went in September 1963 to Bangor Grammar School, where I enjoyed the delights of classes by Irwin Bonar, Maurice McCord and Bruce Greenfield, under-12 rugby at Bloomfield Road, and football and the CSSM in Ballyholme Park in the summer. Life seemed good; I was one of the boys.

I was then sent in September 1964 to board at Ormiston House at Campbell College, where, having completed first year at the Grammar, I was jumped up into the third year. Boarding consisted of three 12 to 16-week terms with one half term break plus two Sunday 'exeats' (i.e. a 12-hour daytime release) each term. This was a bit of shock as I felt I was entirely innocent and the incarceration unjustified. I immediately dispatched a string of carefully crafted letters to my mother, pointing out it was all a big mistake, that I was starving, unloved, hated by everyone around me, often cruelly and viciously punished, and that I was in the final stages of my preparations to run away.

The good news, which I left out of the letters, was that we had three organised sports afternoons each week, Monday, Wednesday and Saturday, with often rugby, cricket or squash matches against other schools twice a week, on Wednesdays and Saturdays. There was also an unsupervised 'sport' for boarders, perhaps unique to Campbell, called 'bugger ball.' It was held in the gym with as many participants as you wanted, usually 10 to 15 on each team.

Gilbert Nesbitt and lifelong friend John Adrain in September 1963 on their first day at Bangor Grammar School. Included are Gilbert's sister Christine and brother Gavin. Below: the picture is recreated more than 45 years later, with Christine inset.

A 'medicine' ball (about the size of a Swiss exercise ball but very heavy and full of who knows what), that each of us would struggle to lift on our own, was placed on the halfway line. The idea was for each opposing team to try to get the ball to touch the wall at opposite ends of the gym. The only rule was that it would have been considered poor form if an opponent died; poor form by the opponent that is.

The bad news was there were Saturday morning classes and there were no girls. Well there was one, the housemaster's blonde daughter, who sensibly didn't fraternise with us. There was also the regular intimidation. Hands in pockets, unbuttoned blazers, being late, no tie, dirty shoes, fighting, not standing in an orderly queue, being too noisy, untidy work books, inadequately prepared homework, reading comics during homework time, or expelling wind at an inappropriate moment, indeed all of the sort of things that made life tolerable for young teenage boys, would result in being given a 'copy.'

This involved the copying out of what then seemed a turgid William Wordsworth poem, printed in elaborate script writing, to a time deadline. The task was to copy out all the words in the exact fancy script. A copy was dispatched as a punishment by a teacher or a collaborating prefect. Some pupils become very adept at doing copies and a black market in copying operated where 'experts' would do other pupils' copies for cash or a share of the cakes or other comforts regularly sent from home. If you were really bad you would get multiple copies or detentions or both, and/ or a caning either on the hand or the rear.

When I was on temporary release from Campbell during the holidays there was fun with three pals, Brian Johnston, William McKee and John Adrain. They had stayed loyal despite me now being an outsider who had both switched to the rugby enemy and had had the temerity to skip an academic year in the process. John and I had been at Connor House together and he had all or virtually all of Elvis Presley's

Hubert Nesbitt (left) and Bertie McConnell.
Spectator picture.

records, which I considered proved John to be particularly mature. I thought his ownership of a 1958 Elvis single to be immense (he would only have been seven at the time) as my first vinyl records started with 1963 Beatles releases. Holiday time revolved around golf, snooker, playing cricket for Bangor Boys, going to the Tonic, illicitly buying and furtively slugging down cans of beer, having unrequited crushes on whatever girls were about, and dreaming about being older, more confident and doing things.

My Mum's cousin Bertie McConnell was an important figure in our family at this time. Bertie had been a talented golfer in his youth and was on the 1935 Grammar School Medallion (under 15) rugby team that won the Medallion Shield (a feat not to be repeated until Dick Milliken's 1966 team). The team had been captained by Maurice Young, who was killed in Italy in 1945. Maurice was the older brother of Elizabeth, who married my father's brother Norman. My cousin Maurice Nesbitt and Maurice Hamilton, son of Horace and Nancy, the motor racing correspondent, journalist and broadcaster, were both named after Maurice Young.

Bertie was blinded at Normandy in 1944 by a booby trap at the age of 23. He visited our house in Waverley Drive every day, walking around the Seacliff Road rain or shine from his confectionery and tobacconist shop at 29 High Street with his guide dog. Bertie would breakfast with us and then he and my dad Hubert would walk back around Seacliff Road and into work.

Whilst sport more than fulfilled the early days at Campbell, once in Sixth Form the reality of institutional boarder existence in a single sex school became much more of a burden. Sport was still a diversion but by this stage it wasn't enough. What I craved was some of the normality going on all over the place in Ballyholme and Bangor that I was being denied. I did my best by showering any girl who spoke to me kindly for more than a minute during the holidays with letters extolling the virtues of my crush but to no avail.

The "Spectator," Friday, 13th November, 1964 5

TONIC THE SHOWPLACE OF BANGOR

Phone BANGOR 5830

To-day and Sat.—Peter Sellers, Paula Prentiss in "THE WORLD OF HENRY ORIENT" (T/Col.), 5.25, 8.40 (Sat. 2.10). Also "ABBOT & COSTELLO IN SOCIETY," 7.15 (Sat. also 4.00)

MONDAY, NOVEMBER 16 FOR SIX DAYS

Doors open 5.30 Continuous 5.40

Matinees Thursday and Saturday Open 2.30 Cont. 2.40

SEAN CONNERY HONOR BLACKMAN GERT FROBE

GOLDFINGER

JAMES BOND 007 BACK IN ACTION

Technicolor Showing 6.00, 8.40 (Matinee 3.25) Also

BASQUE IN THE SUN

Showing 7.55 (Matinee 2.40, 5.15)

CAR PAR :: CAR PARK :: CAR PARK

Saturday night was cinema night for the boarders and we enjoyed all the classics of the time, *The Longest Day, The Great Escape, The Dambusters, Ben Hur, El Cid, The Guns of Navarone*, and, if we were really lucky, a Bond film. Once I got my driving licence I would occasionally park my mum's Riley Elf in Castlehill Road and bunk off for an hour or two to a Bangor pub or join someone else who had temporary access to a car instead of going to the film (our own *great escape*), always being careful to be back before rollcall.

Mostly Sixth Form was about plotting a legitimate means of escape, i.e. getting sufficiently good A-Level grades to move on. The big incentive was that it was made very clear to me that I would be going back if I didn't do the business. This was proving tricky because I had ended up doing Pure and Applied (double) Maths at A-Level without having done O-Level Physics. My third subject, Geography, was being examined under some new Oxford and Cambridge examination board and as we were the first year at Campbell to switch from the Northern Ireland examination board curriculum I sensed the teacher was feeling his way and perhaps adhering too closely to his previous years' Northern Ireland course notes.

Luckily I had a pal, Brian White, who was very bright and who I believed had got the plot; Brian let me have a copy of his notes to revise from. Only five of the 18 pupils in the class passed the A-Level course. Brian got the top mark, a B, while I got a C and the two blokes who'd been awarded the geography prizes for the year by the teacher got an E and a 'Fail' respectively. All my pals at the Grammar who did the Northern Ireland examination board geography course got an A!

In September 1969 there were two places left to be allocated in the Law Faculty at Queen's, from amongst those of us who had miserably failed to make the grades, under the clearing scheme. I was given one of them. I had escaped. I had survived. I could leave boarding school and confront reality. The Sixties were over and I could start to work on doing rather than wishing, on fulfilling all those unrealised dreams.

Sport and Entertainment

Roy Kitson
...remembers

BORN in Belfast in 1949, but a resident of Bangor since he was six months old, Roy Kitson counts himself as a Bangorian. He attended Bangor Grammar School, where he played rugby and hockey, but his true love was football. He attended his first game at Clandeboye Park on 9 March 1962, watching Bangor go down to Crusaders in an Irish Cup tie by six goals to two – "surely an ominous foretaste of supporting the club for the next four and a half decades!"

He studied at Queen's University and taught German and French at Belfast High School and then Sullivan Upper School, all the while following the Seasiders through thick and, mostly thin. Roy began to report for the *Spectator* on Bangor's games in 1985, taking over the role from Colin Bateman and experiencing the halcyon days of the John Flanagan and Nigel Best era and three European adventures in four years. Since then there have

TONY NELSON was a local boy from "The Bullring" on the Clandeboye Road, just a few short yards from the football ground. He was a skilful "classical" right winger and, apart from a spell with Glentoran, played for the team from 1964 to 1966 and from 1967 to 1969, during Glasgow Celtic legend Charlie Tully's two spells in charge at Clandeboye Park. In between times, Ralph McGuicken was the man in the Bangor "hot seat."

A real character, Tony was a key member of the side, joining well-known players of the day such as Dubliners Sonny Rice and Eamonn Farrell (father of actor Colin Farrell), as well as inside forwards Jim Emery, Bill Heaney and Teddy Harte, left winger Steve Gnaulati, from Glasgow, central defenders Joe Woods and Brian Boyd, and "man in black" goalkeeper Jack Milligan. Later on he was setting up goals for forwards Jim Herron, Brian Morrison and Jackie Henry.

In 1966 Tony was awarded an amateur international cap against Wales (0-0 in Portadown). Tony was also involved in one of the most controversial incidents of the time, on 11 March 1967, when Ralph McGuicken was manager of the team. The game was a quarter-final Irish Cup match at Clandeboye Park against

Tony Nelson (front row, second from right) when he played for St Comgall's in the early 1960s. Back row (from left): T. Carlin (club leader), J. Elliott, D. McAlorum, J. McManus, H. Harding, D. McWhirter (trainer). Front: E. McMullan, D. Carlin, J. Thompson, J. Morrow (captain), D. Gray, T. Nelson and G. McWhirter.
Spectator picture.

Portadown and Tony delivered a typical inswinging corner.

Everyone in the big crowd, apart from the referee and his linesman that is, saw Bangor centre forward Brian Morrison – a former Portadown player – knock the ball into the goal with his hand. Amidst massive protests and a pitch invasion from the travelling supporters, a goal was awarded, and with Brian Morrison scoring a "hat-trick", Bangor won the tie 4-1. However, three weeks later the Seasiders lost out unluckily by the odd goal in five in the semi-final against Crusaders at Windsor Park.

Playing wide on the right, Tony was primarily a goal maker rather than a goal taker, though he scored an impressive 11 goals in season 1967/68. In total Tony scored 24 goals in his six years with the club.

Perhaps Tony's most notable goalscoring feat was in an Ulster Cup match at Clandeboye Park on Saturday 9 September 1967, when he scored twice in Bangor's 4-1 victory over what was arguably the best ever Glentoran side, under player-manager John Colrain.

been more downs than ups – and, of course, the big disappointment of "enforced relegation" from the Premiership in the season 2008/2009 after waiting for 12 years for the club to regain its top flight place.

Married to Sheila, they have three children: Steven, Philip and Christopher.

Manager Charlie Tully

That win came just four days before the Glens' amazing 1-1 home draw with Benfica in the European Cup. Mind you, the Glens certainly got their revenge three months later, when they hammered the Seasiders 10-1 in a League match at the Oval!

BRIAN MULGREW burst onto the Irish League scene for Bangor in August 1968. Brian, who had previously played for Queen's Park in Glasgow, possessed a remarkable turn of speed and this pace meant he could beat most Irish League defenders in a race for the ball.

Brian Mulgrew

Bangor's tactics were therefore simple but very effective: play the ball up to Brian who would lurk just behind the centre half and he would gather the ball and race for goal, draw the keeper and shoot for the target.

Brian really was a flying machine. He scored on his debut on 3 August at home to Distillery in a game Bangor won 2-1, and in the following nine matches he netted nine times, including a hat-trick in a 4-0 victory over Cliftonville on 31 August, at Solitude. He scored another hat-trick on 23 November 1968, at home to Distillery in the League when Bangor again won 4-3. He and Billy McCamley formed a formidable partnership before McCamley left in November for Scunthorpe United.

Brian continued on his freescoring ways and, by the end of the season, he had netted 24 times. The following season Brian did one better, with 25 goals to his credit. There were no hat-tricks this time round, but he did score two goals in six games.

However, perhaps his best claim to fame was scoring one of the goals which won Bangor their first ever senior trophy, the County Antrim Shield, in the third replay of the final against Ards at Solitude on 22 May 1970. The other scorers in a 3-1 victory were Jim Herron and centre half Ivan McAllister. Brian had also scored in the 1-1 draw four days earlier.

For the record, the winning team was: Billy Irwin,

Harry Creighton, Bertie Nesbitt, John Kennedy, Ivan McAllister, Paul ("Snowy") Murphy, John Cochrane, Stanley Gregg, Brian Mulgrew, Jim Herron, Brian Morrison, sub Tommy Craig and manager Charlie Tully. Scorers were Herron, Mulgrew and McAllister.

Football writer Roy Kitson.

Unfortunately, Bangor fans were not to see much more of Brian's scoring exploits, for on 24 October 1970, in a match at home to Coleraine, Brian broke his leg. He scored his last goal for the Seasiders in a 3-0 away win against Crusaders, and that was the end of what had promised to be a marvellous partnership up front with Brian Morrison, who had signed for Bangor that summer. Brian did try to make a comeback, but the injury had robbed him of his electrifying burst of speed off the mark. In total Brian scored 57 goals for Bangor.

Bangor FC players celebrate their victory in the County Antrim Shield competition at the end of the 1969/70 season. *Spectator* picture.

Dick Milliken
...remembers

Spectator picture.

DICK Milliken captained the successful Bangor Grammar School Medallion and 1st XV teams before continuing his rugby career at Queen's University, Belfast. He played for Ulster and Ireland and was a member of the 1974 British Lions tour to South Africa, playing in all four Tests in that unbeaten tour. His career ended after a serious ankle injury at the start of the 1975 season. A graduate of Queen's, he is a Chartered Accountant by profession.

I WAS 11 when I had my first introduction to the Ulster Schools Cup and the interest it generated in the local community. I was playing football in Ballyholme Park on a cold Saturday afternoon in February 1962, when two elderly women stopped and enquired how Bangor Grammar School had fared against Rainey Endowed in the quarter-finals of the prestigious competition.

Coming from a sports mad family, excluding rugby that is, I was totally unaware of the outcome but one of my pals was able to provide a detailed report on how Bangor had been narrowly defeated in the final few minutes. I was certainly impressed by the interest those women had shown in a Schools Cup match and their obvious disappointment at the outcome.

That September I started at Bangor Grammar and, with 90 other First Formers, I played rugby every Monday afternoon at either Ward Park or Bloomfield. Under the guiding hand of Jimmy Welch, and with the determination of headmaster Randall Clarke to put Bangor Grammar on the rugby map, the team's performance in that quarter-final at Rainey had been the best to date, and had provided huge encouragement to all involved with rugby at the

Bangor Grammar School's equalising try at the Ravenhill final in 1969 is scored by Billy Kirk. *Spectator* picture.

school. Indeed, it also captured the imagination of many of the townspeople of Bangor.

The school's 1962 intake had brought together a talented group who were very excited by the rugby momentum that was so evident. An inauspicious U13 season, in our second year, hinted at what was possible, but it was the U14 season that saw a decided improvement, with successes being recorded against some of the leading schools, including Coleraine Inst. and Belfast Royal Academy.

The year after that, 1966, we won the Medallion Shield, a mini-Schools Cup for under 15s, defeating Rainey Endowed in the final. It was only the second time the school had won the competition, the previous victory having occurred in 1936! That momentum was definitely building.

The following year the 1st XV lost only once, to a Rainey side that had been undefeated all season and

Bangor Grammar School headmaster Randall Clarke celebrates the Schools Cup success in 1969 with team captain Dick Milliken.
Spectator picture.

would beat Methodist College Belfast in the final. Our match against Rainey was a closely fought encounter, played at Ward Park on a crisp February afternoon with spectators lined six-deep around the pitch.

The 1967-68 season was steady but Bangor Grammar did not build upon the previous year, other than to blood some of the players who had enjoyed Medallion Shield success. Defeat in the second round to Campbell College, again the eventual winners, was a disappointment, but it was the 1968-69 season that gave the school, and the town, that long anticipated first Schools Cup success. The same players who had won the Medallion Shield in 1966 were now in their final year at the school and they provided the nucleus for the 1st XV.

Victories against Orangefield, Annadale and Rainey led to a semi-final clash against one of those long-established rugby schools, Coleraine Inst. A packed Ballymacormick witnessed Bangor Grammar's first ever participation in a semi-final. The *County Down Spectator* subsequently reported a famous victory

Dick Milliken on the way to scoring a try for the British Lions in South Africa (1974).

Dick Milliken in action for the British Lions during the 1974 tour of South Africa. Included are Andy Ripley, Fran Cotton and Sandy Carmichael.

by the huge margin of three points to nil! Plenty of action photographs by Ian Alexander reflected the tense struggle, with a determined rearguard action by Bangor winning the day.

The team's prospects against the mighty Campbell College in the final became the main topic for discussion in local shops, offices and homes during the 10-day build-up to the final. Shop fronts the length of High Street and Main Street were bedecked with blue and yellow banners and messages of good luck. Even the *Ireland's Saturday Night* and *News Letter* did extensive features on the school and the team's prospects in the big match.

The Ulster Schools Cup is one of the oldest competitions in world rugby and the tradition of

The Royal Hotel, venue for a pre-match light lunch for the team. *Spectator* picture.

playing the final at Ravenhill on St. Patrick's Day made it one of the great social occasions in the Ulster sporting calendar, attracting capacity crowds of 18,000. Naturally the entire school was shipped en masse to Ravenhill, complete with banners, flags and other paraphernalia. Glenlola Collegiate even gave its girls a half-day holiday to add some glamour to the occasion! The centre of Bangor was like a ghost town, with local people clearly heeding the banner headline on the front page of the *Spectator*: "All Roads Lead to Ravenhill."

After the team had met at the Royal Hotel for a light lunch, a group of very nervous schoolboys received a wonderful send-off from the many well-wishers who had gathered outside. Numerous were the stories of Old Boys travelling back from England and Scotland, and indeed further afield, for reunions in Belfast prior to travelling to Ravenhill; all were a source of great inspiration for the team.

Blustery conditions on an overcast day were hardly conducive to a free-flowing rugby match, but after a hesitant start Bangor Grammar emerged as 6-3 winners with a penalty in the final few minutes. Celebrations in Bangor over the following few days made the team members feel very important. The match itself, along with a civic reception and another organised by the school, enjoyed extensive coverage in the *Spectator*. With a half-day holiday being granted in honour of the achievement, the 1st XV were particularly popular with the rest of the pupils!

Bangor was much smaller then and there was a great feeling among the players of representing not just the school but also the town. The achievement was deemed all the greater because Bangor had beaten Campbell College, for so long a nursery for Ulster and Irish rugby. It began a long period when Bangor

Dick Milliken pictured at Lansdowne Road, Dublin, in 2006, on the day of the last ever match there, with wife Heather, sons Robbie and James and daughters Jenny and Claire.

Grammar was widely acknowledged as a great rugby school and the cup win also coincided with a golden period for Bangor Rugby Club, which went on to became one of the best in Ireland. Times may since have changed but that sense of community interest and support remains a great source of pride for all those involved in rugby at Bangor Grammar School back in 1969.

Adrian Walsh
...remembers

ACCLAIMED in the mid-Sixties by *Spectator* Editor Annie Roycroft with the words "if he decides to make the stage his career, he is assured of a future," Adrian Walsh was working as a professional stand-up comedian in England by the time he was 22.

Working over the years with such international stars as Glen Campbell, Neil Sedaka, Petula Clark, Gladys Knight and the Pips, Shirley Bassey and Barry Manilow has made Adrian into one of the most sought after comedians in Great Britain. He has been involved in all aspects of the media, including theatre, cabaret, conferences, product launches, and after dinner speaking. He has also appeared extensively abroad, including Europe, America, Canada and Africa.

He is particularly at home with both British and American audiences, making him very much in demand to work on cruise liners all over the world. Adrian has made over 300 television appearances,

I WAS 11 when the Sixties began and, although we didn't realise it then, I now know it was a time of new beginnings for us all. The generation before us had come through the war, and although I never experienced rationing, my older brother Charlie certainly did and he used to tell me about it.

We thought it was all milk and honey in the Sixties, although it wasn't really, except in comparison to what had gone before. It was a time, before television gained in popularity, when everyone would sit in the kitchen, in a circle, and listen to the radio – as if that made a difference!

It was a time when people didn't carry the troubles of the world on their shoulders. Nowadays, with 24-hour news channels, you know what's going on everywhere. We had a chance to grow up in an age of innocence in which we were more interested in football or what was going on at school. There wasn't a world outside Bangor as far as we were concerned.

Of course, like everyone else, I can remember hearing about President Kennedy's assassination in November 1963. We were coming home from the Boys' Brigade – I was in 1st Bangor at that time. We'd stopped at Forte's on Abbey Street for chips and had just got our order when someone told us. I can remember the overwhelming sense of disbelief among the young people.

The cinema was another big thing for the young people of Bangor. I remember the Tonic, the Queen's and the Adelphi. The town also had two great dance halls in the mid-1960s, Milanos and Caproni's. My mum worked in Caps and I remember being allowed in when I was about 11 to see Chubby Checker playing there. I sat in a chair at the side of the function room and fell asleep. When I woke up and found out he'd already been on the stage and was long gone I was devastated.

most recently as a regular on *Today with Des and Mel*, along with a remarkable 14 appearances at the world famous London Palladium. He is constantly travelling abroad, giving talks to the world's largest corporations and has built a reputation where he is known as 'The Giant of Corporate Entertainment.'

Some great names appeared in Bangor, including Roy Orbison and The Kinks at Milanos. That was when I was going out with Vivienne (Porter) who became my wife – we were married in the early 1970s.

As far as my own career is concerned, I was entertaining youngsters at children's parties at the age of eight. I also got great encouragement from *Spectator* Editor Annie Roycroft who wrote about a 6th Bangor Boys' Brigade display in the Dufferin Hall, where I performed a double act with a lad called David Drury.

A large contingent of my dad's family lived in New York. His youngest brother, my Uncle Billy, would come over from time to time. He was one of the funniest men I ever met and he introduced me to the great American comedians like Billy Cosby, Alan King and Don Rickles. I also had *The Stage* magazine delivered to Bangor, at a time when most people hadn't even heard of it.

The young comedian on the verge of stardom.

By the mid-60s the local entertainment scene was really opening up. I can remember the Imperial on Main Street, working with Trevor Kelly and his band, and making my debut there. I also have fond memories of going on to work in Belfast nightclubs like the Appleton Rooms, the Intercontinental, the Trocadero, the Piccadilly Line and the Abercorn. Belfastman Jackie Rae, who was compère at the Talk of the North in Manchester, worked with me at the Piccadilly Line. He told me I had a lot of bottle for my age but I needed to get to England. He said: 'If you work here for the rest of your life you will become a big fish in a small sea. You need to stretch yourself.' He later came to see me when I was doing a show with the Donaghadee Male Voice Choir at the new Technical School in Castle Park, I did the first half and they did the second.

Adrian Walsh with his wife Vivienne, son Callum and daughter Danielle.

Towards the end of the decade I made it through to the final of a *Stairway to Stardom* competition at the Grove Theatre in Belfast. The prizes included £100 and an audition with the BBC but I didn't win anything. Comedians rarely did in those days. The difference was that I wanted to do it and to keep doing it. You can imagine the pride I felt some years later when I returned to the Tonic Cinema, in my own home town, to appear in shows with Val Doonican and with Cannon and Ball.

Paul Donegan
...remembers

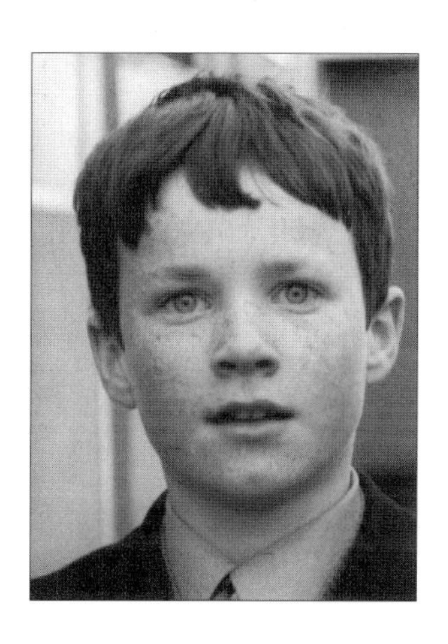

PAUL Donegan was educated at St Comgall's PS, Brunswick Road, Bangor (1962-69), St Patrick's College, Knock (1969-1976), and Queen's University, Belfast (1976-1979). He is married to Zoe and they have four children: Emily, Ptolemy, Evie and Imogen. He owns and operates Donegan's Bar and Restaurant, High Street, and the Royal Hotel and Windsor Bar, Quay Street, all in Bangor.

ONE of my earliest Bangor memories is of the winter of early 1963. My family were living in an apartment, or flat as it was called then, on the third floor above my father John's pub, The Windsor, on Quay Street. I remember watching a succession of Council lorries arriving to tip snow off the North Pier.

I'm pretty sure this was also the year I got a remote control fire engine for Christmas. Not wireless radio-controlled, of course, but connected by wire to a handset – actually a plastic cylinder containing batteries with a steering wheel on top. But what a fireman I was!

This early interest in fire prevention could explain the charming habit I had of eating unusual foodstuffs such as the tufts on my mother's favourite candlewick bedspread... and coal. Coal was not only an occasional and messy source of nutrition, but also of fascination for me from my elevated bedroom window. I loved watching the coal boats coming into the Central Pier. I so wanted to be the man who controlled the huge metal grab that swung over and then sank its teeth into the belly of each vessel. And if I had been, I certainly wouldn't have spilled as much. I suspect the crane driver and the lorry drivers all had relatives living in

The Windsor in the Sixties.
Spectator picture.

the vicinity of the pier since each evening women would arrive and quickly fill their shopping bags with the coal that littered Quay Street.

I also remember women collecting coal along the beach at Queen's Parade. I'm convinced they were actually men in disguise and that their shopping bags were fashioned in the shipyard, because as one who has gnawed through a few hundredweight, I know how heavy it is!

The beaches were my playground. I loved running the gauntlet of the waves along the narrow path at the base of the Queen's Parade sea wall and, in winter when the tide was in, doing the same along Queen's Parade itself. I loved walking there after a good storm to see what had been thrown up by the waves: seaweed, starfish, sand and, of course, coal. At low tide venturing too far up the tunnels that discharged into the bay was not advised. It quickly got very dark, very slippery and very smelly and one's over-active imagination created all manner of ghouls to avoid.

My other outside playground was Barry's Amusements. Although I had no money to play any of the machines, I watched others spend theirs. Who could forget the Electrocutioner, the Hangman or the Guillotinist? Or the shove-a-penny machines? Or the laughing policeman? Or the Ava Gardner and other Hollywood lovelies machine? Or the "What the butler saw" contraption? Or the ghost train?

But most memorable and most intimidating was proprietor Minnie Delino, she of the thousand keys. I would have crawled up one of the aforementioned tunnels all the way to Ward Park rather than cross Minnie!

Minnie Delino with a Barry's ice cream cone in each hand and the famous keys hanging over her left arm. Included is Joan Piper in the van. Picture courtesy of Patrick Byrne.

But then my life changed. We moved from our flat to Ranfurly Avenue. It couldn't have been easy for my mother hauling me and my siblings and the necessary provisions up three flights of stairs. We now had our own private garden and the road to play in (hardly any cars in those days). Across the road were the derelict

Interior views of Barry's Amusements courtesy of John Scully and www.bangorlocal.com.

buildings of former school Garth House. Days were spent climbing trees and having adventures among the old buildings and grounds. My neighbours were the Parr family. Their two boys were Nicholas and Timothy and we had great fun being James Bond or John Wayne, or acting out the next instalment of the short serial films that would have preceded the main feature at the Queen's or Tonic.

A school trip would have meant a walk to Pickie Pool, where if you hadn't previously learnt to swim, you got the Davy Troupe method: a rope was tied under your arms and you were thrown in. If you appeared to be in difficulty, Davy would have hauled on the rope to keep you above the water, but only if you kept your arms and legs moving! Summer at Pickie was great... if you could swim. I used to envy the boys and the girls who could reach the raft outside the pool. I so wanted to do harm to the boys who entertained the girls with their diving abilities. One day I actually walked home from Pickie with a girl! It was a very warm day so she was bare-foot. As luck would have it, however, our relationship ended as abruptly as the dog poo that squelched between her toes.

There were lots of great characters who visited the Windsor for a drink. There was the artist Colin Middleton and wife Kate; Jimmy Heatrick, whose job was to secure the Council public toilet facilities; Jimmy Woods, who owned the then Redcliff Hotel and who hardly ever lost a game of dominoes, and Jim Fleming, who had a barber's shop on High Street. My Dad took me to Jim for my first haircut. He had two huge chairs with red leather upholstery, which he would lower or raise with a foot pedal. For young boys he had a seat that straddled the arms of the chair. It was also my first and only experience of Brylcreem.

I mostly enjoyed working in the bar as a boy but my sisters and I hated the Twelfth. We always felt intimidated by the anti-Catholic songs sung by the bandsmen after a few drinks. We couldn't wait for

Paul Donegan outside the Royal Hotel and The Windsor.

them to go.

Another regular was Billy Caulfield whose rowing boats vied with Laird's Boats for the summer hire business. But the biggest character in The Windsor was undoubtedly my own Dad. He appeared to know absolutely everybody. And he took absolutely no nonsense; the original exponent of zero tolerance!

Or was that Minnie?

Co Down Spectator reporters have their say

Annie Stephens (née Roycroft)

...an introduction

Annie Roycroft (now Mrs Stephens) with a newly-printed copy of the *Spectator*.

AFTER some 42 years with the *Spectator*, interspersed for nine months as a clerical officer with North Down Rural District Council, Annie Roycroft retired in 1983 to marry a man she knew for 35 years – her cousin Joe Stephens, a Cork businessman whose wife had died five years previously. Annie took with her to Cork a portable typewriter, replaced first with a word processor and then with a computer.

Encouraged by her husband she continued to write – but only in a voluntary capacity. A weekly 'Column from Cork' appeared in the *Spectator* for some time, as well as church reports in her local diocesan church magazine and the *Church of Ireland Gazette*. She has written two books. *Memoirs of a Scribbler* made money for two causes – the St John

BANGOR in the Sixties continued to flourish, as a residential town and tourist resort. It was for me much the same as in the previous decade, in that I was still engrossed in the production of a new *Spectator* each week.

In those halcyon days before the onset of the Troubles, events such as Royal visits warranted only the same extent of security as would apply in any other part of the United Kingdom. I recall particularly the visit to Bangor in 1961 of Queen Elizabeth and Prince Philip, with their children Prince Charles and Princess Anne, in the Royal yacht *Britannia*. Crowds welcomed them at Bangor Harbour and at Bangor and Holywood Town Halls. While *Britannia* acted as flagship at the Royal Ulster Yacht Club regatta, the Royal couple had afternoon tea in the clubhouse. The children had been whisked off to a secret destination.

It was the Seventies before there was another Royal visit to the Province. This was also in County Down – but at Hillsborough Castle amidst tight security. There the Queen conducted an investiture. Among recipients of the OBE was a Bangor man she had met on her previous visit – Cllr Bertie McConnell, who became Mayor of Bangor and a Member of Parliament at Stormont. Blinded in the war, he was the first person to have a guide dog in Northern Ireland, and was given the Freedom of Bangor. An unforgettable character, he refused to regard blindness at a handicap.

To come down to a personal note, the Sixties marked my graduation from bike to car. I bought a new Austin A35 for £480 after going on a waiting list for it, in the same way as I had to wait some years previously for a new bicycle – a green Raleigh Superb – which cost £23.

How did I land a job which gave me the privilege of reporting functions ranging from these Royal visits to more ordinary, yet equally enjoyable, events? You can blame Hitler and a comma or two.

I was 15 and attending the local Municipal Technical College. The time was approaching to look for work. My mother spotted a *Spectator* advertisement looking for an office junior. She was anxious that I find work in Bangor, as bombs had fallen in Belfast. (Indeed Bangor also had been bombed, but at least I would be near home – an important factor in view of the black-out in force).

Candidates were given a shorthand and typewriting test by long-time Editor Harry Gaw. I learned subsequently why I was selected. D. E. Alexander, founder and proprietor, had a look at the transcripts and said: "Take that one – she has the commas in the

Annie with successor Jo Bannister in 1983.

Ambulance Brigade in Bangor and the St Luke's Home in Cork. On the strength of this book she was asked to write a history of that Cork home. Entitled *Luke Here!*, it was not intended to make a profit but merely put on record 125 years of caring at a remarkable institution. In the event it also made money for the Home.

Now an octogenarian and a widow – Joe and Annie spent 21 happy years together – she still enjoys occasional visits to relatives in Bangor and is kept abreast of the local news through the *Spectator*, which arrives each week by post, courtesy of the Directors.

"I miss Joe, but he has left a wonderful legacy in his children and grandchildren," states Annie. "Without their love and support I would be lost."

right places." Little did Mr Alexander think that not only he but also two succeeding generations of the family would be lumbered with me! (A fourth generation is now involved in the business. If this is not a record, the fact that since its foundation in 1904 the *Spectator* has never missed a weekly publication despite breakdowns, strikes, stoppages and massive changes in methods of production, is surely worthy of note).

Shorthand and typewriting were vital skills for even the youngest in the office. It was December 1941 and the two reporters were serving in World War II. The only way Mr Gaw (physically unfit to serve in the Forces) managed to keep the show on the road was by dictating his shorthand notes and having them typed by one of the three girls in the office. For example, the morning after Mr Gaw had attended a Tuesday evening meeting of Bangor Borough Council he would dictate his report before dashing to Bangor Petty Sessions; then he would dictate the court reports before, in all probability, going to a Wednesday night meeting and repeating the procedure next day.

This gave me practice for my Gregg Shorthand at a time when I was attending night classes to acquire the RSA Certificate for 120 words per minute. It also afforded an insight into the journalistic side of the newspaper business – more attractive to me than attending the counter and taking in advertisements, or bookkeeping which at that time preceded the computer age. I submitted news items and contributed reports on my interests at the time, from church matters to hockey, tennis and the St John Ambulance Brigade.

It was a decade later – when the war was over, newsprint was derationed and the *Spectator* was set for expansion – before I was reluctantly transferred to the Reporters Room. No member of the fair sex had been there before. There were worries on how a woman would cope with covering evening meetings and returning to the office late at night to despatch news items to the daily papers. In fact, I loved the work, and a few years later I found myself in the editorial chair.

I took seriously the duty of choosing and training apprentice reporters. They were required to undergo a six-month probationary period, and if things proved satisfactory to both parties they were expected to remain for a further three years before going further afield – mostly to the Belfast papers, the BBC or UTV. Most have made their mark in writing or broadcasting in one form or another. Two, Joy (Jo) Bannister and Colin Bateman, are successful novelists. Two, Jack Ledgerwood (who had a successful career in London) and Philip Conaty (who went to Belfast) have died, both too young. John Savage made the short journey to his home town of Newtownards and became Editor of the *Newtownards Chronicle.* Barry Price has been to London and back and I met Ann-Marie Hillen (Mrs Foster) in the *Spectator* Printing Works recently when she was supervising a publication of hers. These are random examples of *Spectator* trainees.

One promising young Bangor man escaped my clutches. When Terence Bowman, author of this book, was considering journalism as a career I enjoyed chatting to him. I knew his parents, grandparents and an uncle, and knew of two other uncles who made the supreme sacrifice in the Second World War. Terence chose to do his training a little farther from home, but still in his native county. On completion of his three years with the *Mourne Observer* I asked if he would consider joining the *Spectator.* He elected to stay where he was, and there occupies the position of Editor with distinction. I look forward to reading his *Bangor in the Sixties,* and admire his ability and energy to produce a book while editing his *Observer* in the shadow of the majestic Mournes.

Bob Templeton

...remembers

AFTER "mind-numbing" office jobs in linen and shipbuilding between 1957 and 1961, Bob Templeton served on the editorial staff of the *Spectator* from 1961 to 1965, reaching the position of senior reporter. He moved to the *Belfast Telegraph*, remaining there until 1969, when he joined the publicity department of Short Bros. in Belfast for a short time. From 1970 until his retirement in 1995, Bob was on the Government Information Service team. A further two years, 1996-1997, were spent in PR consultancy.

THE Swinging Sixties. It was to be the decade of change with mini-skirts, women's liberation, drugs, sexual freedom and rock 'n' roll.

But back in 1961 all of that was a long way off. Bangor Mayor Charlie Valentine was in a slightly embarrassing spot. He had turned up at an official event, albeit a minor one, without his chain of office. Something about it being lost. Actually misplaced.

Watching the proceedings as a very recently appointed junior reporter in the *County Down Spectator*, I thought little about the absence of the chain. But Annie Roycroft, my Editor, saw it differently. A mayor on an official engagement without his appropriate regalia – and believed lost at that – was news in Annie's eyes.

And so it proved. The missing chain ensured the event got a lot more publicity than it would have merited. Clearly, I had a lot to learn about news.

Though a Holywood boy, this was the start of my second spell in Bangor. As a beneficiary of a new Education Act in the late 40s, I had won a place at Bangor Grammar School in 1951, although I had always thought that grammar school was for kids who lived on Drives, Avenues and Crescents, not Streets.

Chips on shoulders even then.

Compared to Holywood, Bangor seemed like a metropolis. It had busy streets, shops galore, parks, a swimming pool and amusement arcades. And then there were the cinemas. The plush Tonic, the long, narrow Adelphi, the slightly seedy Queen's and the Astor. They became my alternative centres of learning, where I learned how the wars were won, how the Wild West was tamed, and how easy it was to fall in love with the likes of June Haver and the more earthy Rhonda Fleming. They were soon to be replaced by a couple of girls at the Hamilton Road Methodist Church Youth Club. Sad to say, it was one-way traffic.

Bob Templeton (left) on an early Sixties assignment with photographer Ian Alexander.

In June 1957 the final bell rang. School was out and as far as I was concerned Bangor was behind me, until my *Spectator* appointment. Another great learning experience had begun, under the guiding hands of Annie Roycroft and Roy Shephard.

The *Spectator* was very much the viewing point and a mirror of what went on in the town. There was the gravitas of the Council meeting amid the hot air and the weekly courts where Resident Magistrate John Long dispensed justice to the stream of wrongdoers who came before him every Wednesday. Then there were the Boys' Brigade displays, garden fetes and a seemingly endless round of bowling club annual dinners – always chicken and ham – where they talked endlessly about their 21 ends. All of it backed up by the births, deaths and marriages. The lifeblood, so to speak, of any thriving town.

Life during my four-year spell as a *Spectator* reporter was not without its lighter moments. Like being perched on the edge of a bed taking notes for an obituary from a newly-widowed woman, with her late husband stretched out on the bed beside me; or being denounced from the stage for an uncomplimentary review of a performance by either Bangor's drama group or the operatic society.

Sadly, probably inevitably, many of my landmarks have gone. The Tonic, the Queen's and why could the Widow's pub not have survived? The Saturday night dances at Caps are but a memory of perspiration and glow, romance and rejection, flirtation and frustration, though I do know of a Caps couple who made it through to a golden wedding anniversary.

But what better memory of Bangor can there be than the Saturday night promenaders on Queen's Parade? Men in sports jackets and open-necked shirts and attractive girls in frocks. The sun always seemed to shine. And above the babble could be heard the soapbox specialists delivering their testimonies with warning about the evils of drink and gambling and other wicked activities. Their salvation always seemed to be preceded by a hell of a good time.

O Happy Days!

PS What of Bangor swinging in the early 60s? Well, there were rumours, but only rumours, of car key parties. Anyhow, I didn't have a car.

Bob Templeton today.

Spectator staff members at a Christmas party in the early Sixties.

Roy Shephard
...remembers

From left: *Spectator* colleagues Roy Shephard, Dougie Boal, John Gore, Jim Gore and Ian Alexander. *Spectator* picture.

WHEN I look back on my years in the *Co. Down Spectator*, there was one aspect of the job that gave me the greatest pleasure, which is why I say to Bangor Amateur Operatic Society – thanks for the melodies!

There is also one aspect of the music scene which makes me sad – the lack of a proper concert hall. The selling of the Little Theatre in Central Avenue, so long the home of Bangor Operatic, was both a milestone and a millstone. It marked the end of an era, but also the beginning of a nomadic existence, which made it extremely difficult to keep the show on the road.

But keep it they have and after 90 years they can still pack them in, in their home from home, the Parish Centre, on Brunswick Road. Grateful as I'm sure they are for the use of this fine hall, it lacks the facilities, the special ambience, the camaraderie of that old home, with its bar, its scene-building facilities, somewhere to

ROY Shephard began his career on the now defunct *Armagh Guardian* under Editor Charles Trimble and one and only reporter Jack McNally. W. D. Flackes, the legendary BBC political correspondent, began his career there too. After four or five years Roy moved to Bangor, where he got the senior reporter's post just vacated by fellow Armachian Jim Gray, who became district reporter for the *News Letter*. Apart from the usual run-of-the-mill markings, Roy covered Bangor's soccer fortunes, but the real pleasure came from his association with the Bangor Amateur Operatic Society.

After another five years, Roy went to the *Belfast Telegraph* as a news sub-editor, later moving to features, where he compiled the television listings in the days long before camera-ready TV pages were bought in. Roy became assistant features editor, working on a wide range of subjects away from hard news, designing pages. It was

Roy Shephard pictured prior to his retirement from the *Belfast Telegraph.*

meet and enthuse.

However, while it may lack such facilities, it still has a core of seasoned officers and performers who have shared their enthusiasm and fired up the ambitions of many new young players, keen to tread the boards. Perhaps one day a more enlightened Council will remedy the situation and provide a theatre, not just for the Operatic Society, but for all musical talent in the borough.

In the meantime, I can take a nostalgic look back at the halcyon days, when Bangor Operatic was a force to be reckoned with on an All-Ireland basis, at the Waterford International Festival of Light Opera, which Bangor first entered in 1961, two years after the Festival began.

In the first 18 years Bangor won the International Trophy (for first place) twice; the Denny Shield for second place four times, and the Phoenix Shield for Best Irish Society three times. They came fourth twice, winning the Swift Shield, and notched up 39 individual awards, along with 26 certificates of merit.

Reading the roll of honour creates flashbacks to great performances by great artistes. There was Evelyn McCall in *Guys and Dolls,* who was a great comedienne, winning awards in *The Boy Friend* and *Calamity Jane.*

I can still visualise the late great Larry McCoubrey in *The Music Man,* a wonderfully colourful show, led by a wonderful, colourful character. Sadly Larry, a BBC presenter, died before he could fulfil his full potential. Sad, too, that great players like John McBurney, the singing milkman, whose friendship I valued, have also passed on.

during this time he also became a TV critic and reviewer, and covered Opera House shows too, following up the interest inspired by the Bangor Operatic Society.

He spent more than 30 years in the *Telegraph,* for the final few years editing 'Letters to The Editor.' Even in retirement, Roy kept his finger on the pulse, working two days a week subbing back on the *County Down Spectator.* And he could be found at the sports desk in the *Telegraph* at the weekend, subbing sport for the morning edition and *Ireland's Saturday Night.*

Another was George Smyth, whose friendship I especially valued. Versatile George, a Northern Ireland Railways engineer by day, won awards in shows such as *How To Succeed in Business Without Really Trying*, and particularly in *Guys and Dolls*, as well as *South Pacific*.

But it was in the annual pantomime that George really came into his own as a great Dame. In panto George could indulge his penchant for ad-libbing, which often earned him the wrath of fellow actors and actresses. He was a wonderful companion, and later I enjoyed his company when we were Churchwardens at the time the foundation stone of St Gall's Parish Church, Carnalea, was laid.

Another name that keeps coming to mind is the majestic Foster Davidson, in the title role of *The King and I*, as well as Billy Bigelow in *Carousel*. Michael McDowell was another fine performer who shared his talents with other societies down the years. Of the leading ladies, Laura Carr was a superb actress as well as singer, as was Florence Loudon.

Michael McDowell as Finch and Florence Loudon, Hedy, in the 1966 production of *How To Succeed In Business Without Really Trying*.

Off stage, people like president Denby Bell played a leading role, as did Jean Hamilton, a hard worker and talented performer too. Also coming to mind are Winston Johnston, Ray Davis, Jack Bennett, Bob Hutchinson, Sheila Ringland, May Spence, Brian Gillespie, Maureen Campbell, Trevor McLucas, several of whom were performers as well as officials.

Some 90 years later, the show is still on the road, despite the difficulties. Long may it continue!

John Gore
...remembers

AFTER moving to California in 1963, John Gore spent eight years in Redondo Beach, working for the *South Bay Daily Breeze*. In 1971 a former colleague recruited him for the *Thousand Oaks News-Chronicle*, a job he held for 10 years. John then moved to Hollywood and trade paper *The Hollywood Reporter*, remaining there until retirement on 9 January 1999, his 62nd birthday.

Since then John has been a tireless charity worker. He has been honoured by the American Diabetes Association, the Cancer Relay for Life Group, the Wellness Community, the Soroptimist International of the Conejo, the Thousand Oaks Rotary Club (a Paul Harris Fellowship Award), the Thousand Oaks Chamber of Commerce (Man of the Year in 1981), Ventura County Supervisors (Man of the Year for the County in 1991), and his home service club, the Kiwanis Club ofThousand Oaks. John has also received the Jackie

I HAD been in the Life Boys, the Boys' Brigade, and a Christian Endeavour group at Clandeboye Road Presbyterian Church, which was run by a man named Cash who operated a pet and garden supplies shop at 82 High Street. There wasn't much going on on Saturday mornings, so with lots of help from Captain Alec Jones, manager of the Tonic Cinema, it was decided to start a weekly Saturday morning show leaning mostly towards teenagers.

We never thought it would become the hit it did! Every Saturday the theatre was filled and we entertained the youth with local groups and local personalities. Teenager Tommy Heyburn became an instant hit with his impersonations of Elvis Presley. And there was another wee lad, 13-year-old Brian Taylor, who sang the big Laurie London hit, "He's Got the Whole World In His Hands." He won a contest for best individual singer. There were local groups featuring singers like the Douglas brothers, of Ava Street, and a young lad called Richard Morrow, whose dad Eric was a successful solicitor in the town.

Professionals just starting out would show up too, and one of them was invited back many times. His name was Brian Rossi and he sang in Belfast

Among his various jobs – all at the same time – John Gore was a driver with Whitehill Taxis. From left: John Gore, Roy Emerson, Wesley Marshall and company owner Percy Marshall at Christmas 1961.

Kennedy Onassis Jefferson Award for community service, and in 2009 he was honoured with the first-ever American Hero Award from Hospice of the Conejo.

He was married to Elizabeth Gabbey, of Clandeboye Road, for 25 years and they had two daughters – Karen and Lesley. They were divorced in 1981 and three years later John met court reporter Sue Hogan on a cruise to Mexico. Married in March 1988, they spend their time travelling, playing golf and volunteering for everything that comes along! John has fought – and beaten – cancer three times in the areas of skin, prostate and bladder, with all now in remission. To this day he misses Bangor and Northern Ireland. Brother Jim and sister Iris still live in Bangor and another brother, Billy, is in South Africa. John has not seen Billy since 1960, but he sees the others whenever he and Sue visit Northern Ireland.

nightclubs. One week we decided to get some publicity for Rossi and the show and arranged for him to "stop" traffic at the top of Main Street. Unfortunately, his crossing of the street in heavy traffic, escorted by over 100 teenagers, got out of control and the police were called.

The funny part was, the officer sent to quell the crowd was big Constable Bob Rankin and the photograph in the next week's *Spectator* showed Bob, in the middle of the street, with his hand raised to wave and a big smile on his face as he looked at the camera. It looked like a posed picture and Bob took a lot of stick for that episode!

Sometime during the Saturday show's great success Van Morrison showed up and he might have been with his group Them, famous for "G-L-O-R-I-A," but I think I'd left for America by then.

Annie Roycroft and the *Spectator* played a big part in the success of the teenage show. Each week, on page 5 of the newspaper, we would feature one of the show's personalities. Tommy Heyburn, a brilliant artist and

Rathgael residents (from left) Raymond Lightbody, John Elliott, John Gore and Bobby Gore, pictured at the top of Helen's Tower at Easter 1960. (John Elliott went to Canada, John Gore to California and Bobby Gore to Australia, while Raymond still resides in the same Rathgael home he lived in when the picture was taken).

painter, was featured amongst others. We even had Louise MacDonald and the famous Tonic pipe organ playing requests during the show.

The Tonic as the Sixties came in was the biggest theatre in Northern Ireland. Friday nights for the typical courtin' couple usually took the shape of dinner in the Tonic Restaurant and a double feature afterwards. A mixed grill, or the favourite liver and onions, was half-a-crown and dessert was a box of Cadbury's Roses from the wee confectionery store next door. The other cinemas were the Astor on Seacliff Road, the Queen's on Queen's Parade (the manager in my time was a character named Jack Lightbody who wore a colourful uniform and carried a chair leg up his sleeve to keep order!), and the Adelphi and the Tudor (both on lower Main Street).

The Abbey Press (where I served my apprenticeship) was next door to the Tudor and shared the same toilet facilities. When we finished work at night we'd go next door, sit in the back and watch the current movie. In those days, films changed three times a week so we got to see a lot of new releases!

John Gore today.

Looking back now, almost 50 years later, those were really happy and fun times and often I think about the youngsters who came to scream and shout and behave like perfect teenagers. And we know that, through the Tonic Teenage Show, a lot of them went on to great success in life!

Members of the then newly-formed Bangor Fire Service football team in the early 1960s. Back (from left): Joe Thompson (referee), John Gore, Clive Thompson, Dougie Scott, Roy Emerson, Bobby Emerson, Jim McDowell. Seated: Eric Savage, Bryce Baird, Stewarty Vaughan, Jimmy McAuley, Ean Thompson. Front: Frankie Millsopp and Jack McConaghie (linesmen). *Spectator* picture.

THE COUNTY DOWN SPECTATOR AND ULSTER STANDARD

SHOES

WARNER'S

STRANGFORD SOCKS

CULTRA MANSION DESTROYED

It started as a chimney fire

Local man killed at shipyard

American teenagers here tonight

Tragic accident on way from Dublin

BANGOR MAN DIES IN BLAZING CAR

Received C.B.E. from Queen

Main Street shop realises £14,500

MR. MAY AGAIN

Father was lost at sea

Bangorian promoted

Rodney

Anne Roulston

perfection in BROADER fitting shoes

Van-Dal

WARNER'S

MAIN STREET BANGOR

JOHN Gore not only supplemented his income by working as a taxi-driver around Bangor and district, but he was also a retained fireman. The section leader was Joey Thompson, who ran a small shop in Central Avenue. John recalls those times when he worked with a "great bunch of crazy lads" who fought fires back then before the Troubles.

Leading Firemen included Jack McConaghie (electrical shop on High Street), Roy Emerson (a locksmith from Beatrice Road), Frankie Millsopp (a grocer on Main Street), and Eric Savage (a car mechanic with Marshall's on Abbey Street), while the rank and file included himself and Jimmy McAuley (both worked for the *Spectator*), Bryce Baird (a shoemaker from King Street), taxi driver/ car repair and bicycle shop owner Percy Marshall, George White, Dougie Scott, Stewarty Vaughan (from Rediffusion), Ian Thompson who lived very close to the station on Castle Street, window washer Tucker Beattie and electrician Clive Thompson, who worked for Jack McConaghie.

One fire was a highlight over the years. It was at Cultra Manor, up in the hills on the Bangor side of Holywood. Bangor station got the assist call, which meant things were out of control and help was needed. On arrival, the fire was through the roof, water was scarce, and the only thing was to save surrounding homes. The *Spectator* covered the story with a front page headline that included the words: "It started as a chimney fire!"

Helen Greenaway (née Russell)
...remembers

The teenage Helen Russell with John Lennon at the King's Hall in 1964.
Spectator picture.

HELEN Greenaway (née Russell) commenced her career in journalism with the *Spectator*, as a junior and then senior reporter from the early to mid-1960s. This was followed by the *East Antrim Times*, trainee reporter (1960s); *Belfast Telegraph*, reporter/ sub-editor, 1970s; the *News Letter*, sub-editor/ assistant editor, 1990s; *Newry Democrat*, Deputy Editor, 2007-2008.

IT'S been a hard day's night recalling my days as a junior reporter at the *County Down Spectator* in the 60s – for reasons which will become clear. It was either go straight from school to a pensionable position in the Gasworks or opt for an exciting, lowly paid career in newspapers.

I never regretted my decision. What 17-year-old could forget covering their first formal luncheon as a guest of the Borough Council? Surrounded by dignitaries, a former headmaster welcomes her with the words: "Boy, but she cleans up well." And there was me thinking I was looking ever so chic in my little blue outfit.

There followed months of inputting weddings and obituaries, ensuring festivals and sports results made it to the train in time for the next day's dailies – and that extra bit of pocket money. Life was a constant round of AGMs, church services, Unionist meetings, displays and gymkhanas. I did my time in court and chalked up four solicitor's letters at the first sitting, much to the horror of Editor Annie Roycroft. Fortunately a clarification was sufficient and a lesson was well and truly learned.

Helen Russell meets the Beatles

FACE TO FACE WITH WORLD SHAKERS

'Round the Houses' talk to schoolgirls

CHRISTMAS PRESENTS!!

BRITEROME HARDWARE

ALL PRICE:

SKIRTS WOOL SCARVES SHORTS

SLACKS BELTS and JEWELLERY

ROBERTA'S

MAIN STREET

SCOUT NOTES

TOP TEN

'Come into the parlour'

Off to sea

GALA

In 1963 I was given a weekly column, *Teenage Topics*, which focused on the Tonic Teenage Show. On Saturday mornings the town's young people flocked to watch films and take part in talent competitions. The inspiration behind the weekly event was the larger than life cinema manager Captain A. C. Jones.

The show attracted acts from across Ireland and provided a showcase for local talent. Among the regulars were teenage sensations The Janitors and The Sapphires. Other popular Bangor vocalists included Maureen Swindle, Carol Hopley, Mason Douglas, the well-known singing duo Anne and Jack Chambers, and Anita Matthews, a friend of mine from Ballyholme Primary School days.

Local girl Marilyn McWhirter went on to be the singer with Fred Hanna's Band in the Floral Hall. Young Brian Taylor was another favourite with audiences, while mime artist Tommy Heyburn even merited his own fan club. A record request spot hosted by Colin Barnes and Richard Morrow added to the entertainment.

The first beauty contest since the war was held at Pickie Pool in the 60s. The *Miss TV Post* competition, sponsored by UTV and Bangor

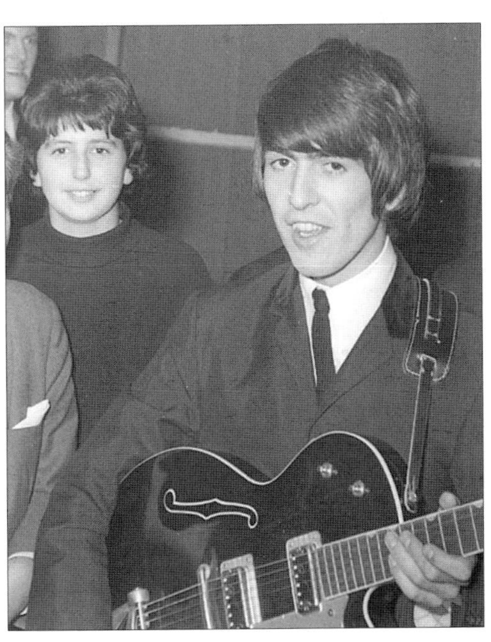

Helen with George Harrison. *Spectator* picture.

Teenage beauty competitions were a highlight in the Bangor summer programme of special events in the mid-1960s. John Trew (right), who later became Editor of the *News Letter*, organised many as assistant publicity/entertainments manager with Bangor Borough Council. He is pictured at Pickie Pool, protecting the bouffant hairstyle of a pretty contestant in the *Miss TV Post* competition.

Borough Council, was the brainchild of Captain Jones and Major J. M. Affleck, Bangor's entertainments manager. It attracted entrants from across Ulster and gave Tonic performers another stage on which to tout their talent.

My 60s highlight was, or rather should have been, an interview with The Beatles. The chance meeting came about when promoter Trevor Kane asked the *Spectator*'s Ian Alexander to take a souvenir photograph of the fab four for the Queen's Court Hotel. Ian kindly took me along on the off-chance I'd get to meet the legends in the flesh.

And backstage at the King's Hall, Belfast, I did just that. I got to interview the Liverpool lads in their undies. I tried to remain 'cool' as they dressed, chatted, joked and prepared to go on stage. But to this day, I truthfully can't remember how the line of questioning went. There

Bangor band The Sapphires were among the acts on the programme for the pantomime 'Snow White and the Seven Dwarfs,' which was presented by the dramatic society of Ballyholme Presbyterian Church in December 1962. Members were Patrick Coghlin, Brian Miller, George Nelson, Sydney Barlow, Billy McClinton and Roderick Alexander. *Spectator* picture.

The Beatles on stage at the King's Hall in 1964, with Ringo's head obscured by his own drum kit. *Spectator* picture.

was the most embarrassed teenager on the planet, talking to, perhaps, the most famous quartet in history. However, despite the blushes, I did manage to get a paragraph or two for the Helen Russell column.

And yes, I do still cringe at my criticism of *A Hard Day's Night*, the group's first film. Another most embarrassing Beatle moment!

Helen Greenaway with daughters Heather (left) and Emma.

Ric Clark

...remembers

RIC Clark was a member of the editorial staff of *Spectator* Newspapers, working in both Newtownards and Bangor, between 1964 and 1968, when he joined the *News Letter* in Belfast as a sports reporter.

After a year there he moved 'Down Under' and served as a news reporter with the *Sydney Morning Herald* and then as political correspondent with the *Brisbane Courier Mail*. Back in Belfast in 1972, he joined the staff of the *Sunday News*, and seven years later he was appointed its news editor.

In 1983 he returned to the *News Letter* as assistant news editor and in 2003 he was appointed news editor. Between 1982 and 2001 Ric was also Ireland correspondent for United Press International, Washington DC.

WITH the exception of Christmas Day the highlight of my year as a youngster was a day trip to Bangor. That was in the Fifties when large families, still struggling through the post-war years and ration coupons, packed into trains and buses and headed to the seaside. A day trip with the annual Sunday School excursion to Ballyholme is still vivid in my mind.

To me Bangor was magical but little did I know then it was to play a vital role in my salad days as a teenager. That all started in 1964, when I applied for a job as a cub reporter with *Spectator* Newspapers. I travelled for my interview by train from the Queen's Quay railway station in Belfast. When I recall that trip the smell of the steam engine and the smoke belching from its funnel still lingers in my nostrils.

I got the job with a grand salary of £2.19s 6d a week. Even with that my father had to subsidise my travel expenses to the tune of 10 shillings a week. I was to start work at the offices of the *Newtownards Spectator,* where I began a sharp learning curve in journalism. It was a baptism of fire, trying to grasp the essentials of not just reporting weekly events but also to face the terror of attending Magistrate's Courts, the Crown

Court and monthly meetings at North Down Rural Council, as well as Newtownards and Donaghadee Councils.

On my very first day reporting at the Magistrate's Court a well known businessman was convicted of drink-driving. As I was leaving the court, after checking I had the correct names of defendants, their lawyers and the wording on the charge sheet, that same businessman confronted me outside and stuffed a £5 note into the breast pocket of my jacket, smiled and said he would appreciate it if I forgot about his case and smartly walked away.

In my panic I imagined myself being charged with accepting a bribe and facing imminent dismissal from my job. A policeman was still on duty at the front door so I handed over the bribe and returned to my office where my Editor instructed me to write up every detail of the case. As I left his office he complimented me on my honesty and said the story would be highlighted as the lead to the courts page. I never heard from that businessman again – and I was never told about what happened to the £5 note.

Relations between the police and the Press in the Sixties bear no resemblance to the present day. It was a time when a reporter could speak directly to any officer involved in an investigation and get "guidance" on condition the officer remained an unnamed source. It was not unusual for reporters to phone the police station and ask for a lift with the District Inspector or Head Constable to a court sitting in Donaghadee or Holywood. It was a reflection of the good cordial relations between the police and the local Press.

Even magistrates had their moments. I recall receiving a phone call in my office from Resident Magistrate Albert Walmsley, who would be sitting on the bench at Comber Court the following day. He asked if I was covering the court could I give him a lift as his own car was out of action. It was only as we drove to the court, strictly observing every rule of the road, he confessed his wife was using the car for

Ric Clark today.

another engagement.

Relationships like that permeated many aspects of life in Bangor and the North Down communities. It was an era when young people lived carefree lives, membership of youth organisations was at an all-time high, and the addiction to showbands in the Caproni's and Milanos dance halls at Ballyholme was the true setting for Saturday night fever. The absence of alcohol and the lack of foul language were just part of the long since lost innocence of the time.

In the summer months Bangor just exploded with an influx of tourists. B&Bs were packed and no matter where you went Scottish, English and American accents were always ringing in your ears. I particularly sympathised with the American tourists who could never understand British currency. I remember watching a couple sitting at the table next to me in a restaurant on Queen's Parade. When they received their bill they were totally confused and didn't know how to count out the cash. They almost confused me as they tried to work out how many pennies made up a shilling, what a half crown was worth – was it worth more than a two shilling coin and what about the threepenny and sixpenny pieces?

In his frustration the man turned to me and asked if I could show him how to make up the total and with that he emptied several handfuls of coins and notes onto the table saying they were so confused they just paid for everything with ten shilling and pound notes. The bag he was carrying was bulging with coins.

"What should I leave as a tip?" he asked.

"I'm sure a sixpence should cover it," I replied.

With that he lifted a handful of coins from the table

and put them onto a saucer saying, "Would that be enough?" and adding: "Do you know if you sorted out your money over here a lot more Americans would come and visit."

I just smiled and after they left the restaurant a disbelieving waitress carried the saucer to the counter where a second waitress stood open-mouthed as she counted the change.

When I paid my own bill I asked the waitress if she was surprised by the tip.

"There was almost a pound there," she smiled.

I'm afraid my tip fell a long way short of that!

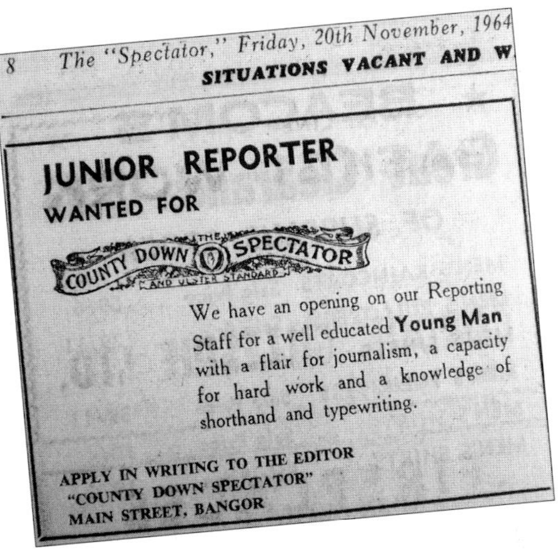
8 The "Spectator," Friday, 20th November, 1964
SITUATIONS VACANT AND W

JUNIOR REPORTER
WANTED FOR
THE COUNTY DOWN SPECTATOR AND ULSTER STANDARD

We have an opening on our Reporting Staff for a well educated **Young Man** with a flair for journalism, a capacity for hard work and a knowledge of shorthand and typewriting.

APPLY IN WRITING TO THE EDITOR
"COUNTY DOWN SPECTATOR"
MAIN STREET, BANGOR

This advertisement seeking a new journalist appeared in the *Spectator* in November 1964 – long before the sex discrimination laws were introduced!

Marion Cortina (née Johnston)
...remembers

Young reporter Marion Johnston (left) with her cousin Noreen Johnston in the *Spectator* offices.

AFTER raising her family Marion spent several years living abroad, mostly in Mexico, and returned some years ago to live in Oxford. She now lives and works near Cambridge.

AS with many people recalling their childhoods, it seemed like the sun was always shining and everyone was happy. I remember Bangor in the Sixties as a golden place before the horror of the Troubles and all that followed. Having moved from the depths of the country to Bangor, I always felt like the proverbial fish out of water, but when my country cousins used to visit they thought me incredibly lucky to live by the sea.

I remember many days spent on Ballyholme Beach, where families camped out for the day with their pitch set up – deckchairs hired from up on the promenade, brightly painted changing rooms in use all day, windbreaks – a most necessary accessory on an Irish beach – and picnics hauled down the steep steps.

Women sat knitting, men slept with their trousers rolled up to knee level, children ran around building sandcastles and, if old enough and brave enough, swam out to the raft. You were very grown up if you were able to do that, returning mottled from the cold of the sea, all pink, red and sometimes blue, to receive rations of lemonade and sandwiches well covered with sand.

The popular Caproni's ballroom. *Spectator* picture.

Living by the seaside with most of the family still in the country meant that throughout summer we had a constant succession of visitors. This usually involved an evening visit (can't remember now if it was Saturday or Sunday) to watch the square dancing at the Marine Gardens at Pickie. I pretended to think this deeply uncool but secretly wanted to be able to dance the Gay Gordons with just as much gusto as the dancers.

CAPRONI'S
BALLROOM : Phone 45 : BANGOR
SATURDAY, 14th JANUARY
THE FABULOUS
CLIPPER CARLTONS
Dancing 8.45—12. Subscription 5/-
★ ★
SATURDAY 21st JANUARY
DAVE GLOVER
B.B.C. T.V. SHOWBAND
★ ★
SATURDAY. 28th JANUARY
THE MIGHTY RHYTHM BOYS
★ ★
COMING SOON
THE GREAT JOHNNY FLYNN

Safety didn't seem to be such an issue then and we frequently went long distances on our bikes. Many a time I would cycle past Caproni's on a summer evening and watch the women in their wide-skirted frocks and dream of being one of them. However, by the time I was old enough Caproni's was old hat and Milanos was the place to go – and mini dresses were the style.

In my short time at the *County Down Spectator* I got to see many groups and solo performers, including Dusty Springfield, The Searchers, The Kinks and Lulu. For some reason Editor Annie Roycroft let me loose on the job of interviewing Lulu in a hotel in Belfast. The sheer terror of finding the hotel almost finished me off before I had even begun, but Lulu turned out to be quiet and rather pleasant and all was going well until the manager of a local showband

Marion Cortina with daughter Claire McCauley.

(whose name I now forget) came over and ranted at me very, very loudly for having rubbished his band the week before in the *Spectator*. He was very tall and I was five foot nothing and I couldn't even get my mouth open to defend myself, such was the tirade. Meanwhile Lulu and friends just sat there in amazement. It was an interview I will never forget. Just to show my total lack of judgment, I thought she would never get anywhere...

My fondest memory of the *Spectator* has nothing to do with interviews but the visits of Paco the dog, who I think belonged to Mr. David S. Alexander. Paco used to launch himself at me in order to be properly hugged and loved as he knew all Bassets should be, but once he hit me so hard I went straight through the cloakroom door which was tightly shut at the time. They are surprisingly heavy dogs and I have craved one ever since.

I realise now that I was most fortunate to grow up in a place full of great natural beauty and with kindly, intelligent people.

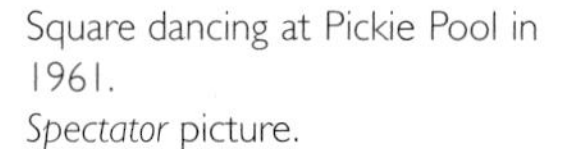

Square dancing at Pickie Pool in 1961.
Spectator picture.

Norma Wilson (née McCormick)
...remembers

Reporter Norma McCormick at the top of the table at a *Spectator* Christmas lunch in 1968, with colleagues Ric Clark, Michael Wolsey and Jack Ledgerwood. Others in the picture include Rena Davidson (now Mrs Warwick Stewart, office), Zella Cavan (bookbinder) and Lydia McNarry (Mrs McMullan, office).

LITTLE did I know when I walked into the offices of the *County Down Spectator* and asked for the Editor, that I was following in the footsteps of the first woman editor in Northern Ireland, if not the British Isles.

I was 16, good at English, and lived in the dream world of writing poetry and short stories. My English teacher at Bangor Technical College, Miss Ferris, advised me to contact Annie Roycroft to see if I could get a job in journalism. That was the day that started a lifetime involvement with newspapers, ending up eventually with a career in advertising sales. Back then it wasn't necessary to study journalism at college; all we needed was a love of English, plus good shorthand and typewriting skills.

My earliest memories are of the noise of the printing press and the smell of the printers' ink. There were no

DAUGHTER of Norman and Jean McCormick, Norma was educated at Trinity PS, Central PS, Bangor Girls' Secondary and Bangor Technical College. After leaving the *Spectator*, she opened the Maggie May boutique at Abbey Street, during which time son Ainsley McCormick Laughlin was born. She later moved to Cookstown with ex-husband Alan, son Ainsley and baby daughter Lois.

After the birth of Alana, she joined the advertising department of the *Mid-Ulster Mail* on a part-time basis. She spent two years with *Car Sport* magazine, but when Morton Newspapers bought over the *Mid-Ulster Mail* she was invited back as deputy advertising manager, followed by further promotion to advertising manager of the *Craigavon Echo* and, two years later, the *Tyrone Times*.

She and second husband

Norman live near Gilford in a converted 300-year-old farmhouse. In total they have five children, including Norman's daughter Alison and son Ian, and seven grandchildren. Other loved members of the family are four white poodles, one Jackadoodle (poodle/Jack Russell mix), three much spoiled cats, four noisy white ducks and three adopted terrapins!

Norma also has two sisters, Mrs. Caroline Cullen, Sister in the Oncology Unit at the Ulster Hospital, Dundonald, and Mrs. Frances Williams, Consultant Pathologist at Derriford Hospital, Plymouth. Nowadays she enjoys making dreams come true by selling property throughout Turkey and she also sells advertising for a friend, Mrs Beryl Bickerstaff, of B&B Media.

ear protectors in those days and I can remember pressing my fingers to one ear, while holding the phone tight to the other, in order to carry on a telephone conversation. I was always fascinated by the way the typesetters hammered the metal text into place, mirror image. They were able to read it as quickly as I could read the paper when it rolled off the press.

We had one of the best classified sections of any newspaper and I would help out in the front office when needed. Many items of furniture in my house today came from those pages. In charge was Miss Caroline Creber, of whom we were all in awe. A tall, thin woman, with white hair tied back in a bun, she had a wonderful Cork accent and was a great teacher of office procedures – everything went smoothly with Miss Creber in charge.

Norma Wilson today.
Picture courtesy of Monica Gorman.

Mr. David S. Alexander, a director of the *Spectator*, was a very imposing man with lots of white hair. He tended to be a bit forgetful and a particular story I remember related to his much loved Bassett Hound Paco. 'Mr. David' tied Paco's lead securely to a nearby lamppost while in deep conversation with a friend. It was dark when he arrived home and his wife Lolita enquired about the dog, which was obviously nowhere to be seen. A car was duly dispatched and I believe Paco suffered no lasting trauma!

My first love was the courts and because I was a good shorthand writer and typist I eventually found myself covering the sittings in Bangor, Newtownards and Holywood. In those days there were no breathalyser tests and the police had to give evidence of the manner in which the accused walked a straight line or if he was able to touch his nose with his eyes closed.

I have fond memories of one Resident Magistrate, Mr. Martin McBirney, whose humanity showed time and time again in the way he dealt with offenders. Some years later, during the height of the Troubles, I was deeply saddened to hear he had been shot dead at his home in Belfast. All the magistrates showed me great kindnesses and were very good at keeping me on the right path!

Then there was the weekly "women's column," when new fashions were highlighted or the latest make-up featured. I wish I was still on the receiving end of those wonderful parcels, most of them sent to me by the head of the Elizabeth Arden department in Robinson and Cleavers. Mrs. Roper Lindsay was the most elegant woman I have ever met.

Mini, midi and maxi skirts, wedges, stilettos, thigh-length boots, laced boots, gypsy skirts and blouses, frills dripping from your wrists, fringes tickling your ankles, leopard skin trousers, long suede coats embroidered with ethnic designs – fashions came and went during my six years at the *Spectator*. As did hairstyles – there was bouffant, the Mia Farrow, short and curly, long and curly, short and straight, long and straight – you name it, we all tried it.

The fashions that had been gracing Carnaby Street made it to Bangor a couple of years later. The place to show them off was the seafront on a Sunday. The "wall" at Queen's Parade was the meeting place for the fashion-conscious of Bangor. Not the most comfortable of seats, but definitely the place to be seen. A new outfit was a must for Saturday nights and Caps and Milanos offered a catwalk for the latest trends in footwear, hairstyles and fashions.

Miss Roycroft was a great mentor and undertook to teach me how to drive – a very necessary attribute for a budding journalist. Her patience was commendable as was the durability of her A35. She had the heart of a lion, considering the first time I did the test I nearly drove into the back of a double-decker bus! Suffice to say I did not have my driving licence when I left the *Spectator*. Quite possibly this experience was why she later insisted on trainees producing a driving licence along with their shorthand and typing certificates!

The *Spectator* was a wonderful place to work and I was pleased to hear in latter years that Miss Roycroft met her soulmate, married and moved to Cork. She was a tremendous role model and loved young people. Through her, many of my colleagues have gone on to make an impact in the world of media and publishing. Being asked to contribute to this book has brought back many happy memories and on a personal level has made me realise that nothing will ever touch the adrenalin rush of press day or the pleasure of seeing what you have written in print.

Cast members – including a young Norma McCormick – from a nativity play presented by pupils of Bangor Girls' Secondary Intermediate School in December 1962.
Spectator picture.

Brian Orr
...remembers

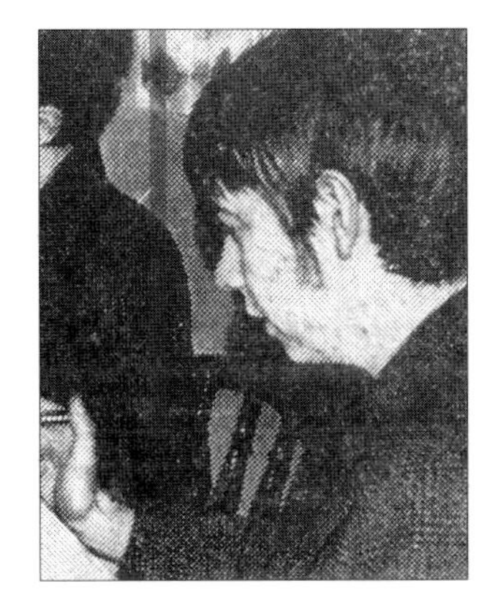

HAVING joined the *Spectator* at 17, in 1968, Brian Orr spent five years in Bangor before leaving for the *Belfast Telegraph* where he was sent to the Derry office, replacing another Bangor native, Richard Lightbody.

Six months later the *News Letter* offered him a reporting job in Belfast. It may have been at the height of the Troubles but for someone in their early 20s, working in one of the world's hot news spots was an experience he would not have missed. Brian considers himself lucky to have met and worked with some of the great characters in Belfast newspapers, such as Ralph Bossence, Tom Samways, Hammy McDowell, Jimmy and Kay Kennedy.

While at the *News Letter* he moved to the sub-editors department at the urging of Cyril Thackway and spent some six years working with chief sub Dick Riddell, "the most original person I have known." There was also the attraction of a four-day week for *News Letter* subs, which gave him

FOR someone who wanted to make his career in news, who took pride in being up to date in current affairs in the mid-Sixties, it was a very humiliating experience to be told of what was then the biggest story to hit Bangor several hours after it happened by a school friend.

It was Peter Gibson who relayed the news to me that December morning back in 1965 as form Lower 4Q assembled in classroom H5 in Bangor Tech's Hamilton House.

"I didn't think you'd be in today," he said.

"Why not?" I asked in my innocence.

"Have you not heard the news?"

"No."

"Your grandfather's shop burned down early this morning," he said.

I was, naturally, stunned and unable to take it all in. Everyone else, however, did seem to be better informed and aware of what had happened a few hundred yards from Hamilton Road at 99 Main Street.

Simon's, a small department store with men's, women's, haberdashery, millinery and soft furnishings sections, was, we in the family liked to think, the best shop in Bangor and surrounding area. Certainly, it sufficient leisure time to pursue his hobby of sailing.

In 1984 Brian married Janet and, rather than work nights for the *News Letter*, he moved back to the *Belfast Telegraph* where he ended his journalistic career as sub in charge of letters. With two children, Niall and Judith, setting out on their own careers, Brian's days are now spent pottering around boats and playing with his new toy, a motorbike. He says: "I hope my children will be as fortunate and blessed as I have been."

clothed and furnished the extended Kane family of Orrs, Stewarts and Spences. It did not, however, belong to my grandfather, George Kane. He was one of the directors and when the owner, William Simon, died, it was my grandfather who took all to do with the running of the shop. And so we all looked on it as 'our shop'.

After the fire it was no more. There was no attempt to rebuild and reopen and for several months after the blaze, my grandfather spent his time winding up the business.

There was, though, a positive side to the disaster. Among the fittings that were salvaged from the inferno and ended up in my granda's garage at Grove Park were several clothes racks, the type of metal frames on castors that held dresses, jackets, suits, etc. There were also the metal base frames of beds, complete with springs.

And here's where my uncle Jim Kane's ingenuity came in. He took the bed frames, bent them at right angles to form seats and then strung them on light chains from the clothes racks. Hey presto! Comfortable, swinging garden seats were emerging from the garage, complete with fitted cushions made by my mother.

For years afterwards the extended family enjoyed summers in their bespoke swinging seats.

You could say this was my introduction to the Swinging Sixties!

After that episode I decided it would be better to pay more attention to the local news. Reading national newspapers in the Carnegie Library, watching documentaries and *Panorama* on TV was not really sufficient to prevent one from being scooped on local issues by school friends. That's where the *Spectator* came in. I decided it would be a great job to report on such events. Editor Annie Roycroft agreed to give me a job during the school summer holidays at the urging of Joe Cairnduff, the head printer at the *Spectator*, whose wife was friendly with my mother. Then, when reporter Ric Clark left, I was offered a full-time job. It was great to be joining the likes of Jack Ledgerwood, Michael Wolsey and Norma McCormick, whose names I had only known before as bylines.

DRASTIC ACTION TO GET MOVE OFF STAGE

HOW MANY GROUPS around to-day would be willing to continue their act for so long that the management would be forced to turn off the electricity to get them off stage?

Not many, but the Move are an exception as they proved on Saturday night (Sunday morning?) at Milanos.

By BRIAN ORR

One of the great perks of the job, at least for a teenager in the Sixties, was free admission to Milanos on Seacliff Road, which attracted some of the biggest names in pop during their British tours. It meant I not only got in free to see the concerts, but also to interview the stars – Tiny Tim, Roy Orbison, The Move and the subject of my greatest pop exclusive, Dave Dee of Dave Dee, Dozy, Beaky, Mick and Tich fame.

It was to the *County Down Spectator* that Dave revealed he had a secret desire to play Hamlet. Some weeks later the *New Musical Express* claimed to have the scoop on Dave's theatrical ambitions. I believe he actually did achieve his ambition but Hamlet won.

Not all encounters with the giants of pop were so productive. When The Move played Milanos I was backstage in their dressing room taking pictures and trying to interview a sullen Roy Wood. His fellow band members were full of the joys of life but Roy just stood in the corner glowering at me. Then there was a knock on the dressing room door. Roy moved to answer it and then turned to me and said there were a couple of girls looking for the *Spectator* reporter. For a few fleeting and heart-stopping moments I really did believe that Yvonne McIlmail (a friend from school) and Linda Shaw wanted to see me and not their pop idols, but I was able to make their night by taking their picture with the group – including the sullen Roy Wood who did actually smile.

Brian Orr today.

Those really were the golden days.

Jo Bannister

...remembers

JO Bannister was born in Rochdale, Lancashire, in 1951. She has also lived in Birmingham, Nottingham and in Bangor.

She left school at 16 to work on her then local weekly newspaper, the *County Down Spectator*. Fifteen years later she was its editor. But by the mid-1980s the growing success of her books on both sides of the Atlantic meant a choice had to be made, and she left journalism to concentrate on her career as a crime novelist.

Her writing, both as journalist and author, has attracted widespread critical acclaim and she has won or been short-listed for a number of provincial, national and international awards, including the Royal Society of Arts Bronze Medal, the Catherine Pakenham Award, the British Press Awards, the Northern Ireland Press Awards, the Ellery Queen Readers' Award and the Mary Higgins Clark Award.

For the past several years she has been among the top 2% of authors

You cannot hope to bribe or twist...
...thank God! the British journalist.
But seeing what the man will do
unbribed, there's no occasion to.
Humbert Wolfe, 1886-1940

I WENT into journalism almost by default. Having hated every minute of school, I needed a job you could do without A-Levels, much less a degree. In the late '60s the best start for a reporter was an apprenticeship with a local paper.

The other entry requirements – five O-Levels and typing – came easily enough, but I struggled with shorthand in an attic room of the Victorian villa on Princetown Road which was then Bangor Technical College. The hundred words a minute I needed seemed impossible. I inched the qualification by remembering what the examiner had said a good two sentences after he'd finished speaking.

It was the only time I ever took shorthand that fast. Most speakers pad out their remarks so much that sticking to the relevant bits removed the need for much speed.

Accuracy *was* important, particularly in court reporting. Bangor Magistrate's Court was held on Wednesday mornings; copy for Thursday's *Spectator* – anything up to 3,000 words – had to be in as soon as possible and anyway by early Wednesday evening. We covered every case heard. It might only be a line for a speeder, a paragraph for someone convicted of careless driving, but every case was recorded for posterity. Occasionally defendants tried to keep their affairs out of the paper, and were astonished that they couldn't buy our discretion.

The nice thing about the *Spectator* was that these young journalists, some of them only 16-years-old, were genuinely trying to do a professional job. We reported fairly and accurately. We valued our reputations. When I returned to the *Spectator* as deputy editor and then editor, we still worked that way. You get, and keep, good journalists by supporting them, and not yielding to vested interests, however unpopular that makes you.

The most important customer of any newspaper is not the advertiser, nor the local Council, nor any other body however worthy or influential. It's the guy who goes into his corner shop and puts down his money in return for thousands of printed words he has no way of verifying. He has to trust that you're telling him the truth. You don't betray his trust to please some local bigwig whose interests might be better served by a judicious realignment of the facts. Not in 19 years as a reporter and editor did I send to print a story I knew or had reason to suspect was untrue.

I wasn't unique in that. We all saw ourselves as performing an important service for our readership. We made mistakes – of course we did – but not many, and never through malice, fear or favour.

I don't think we got the credit we deserved. People's view of journalism was coloured by what they knew about the sink end of Fleet Street. Fleet Street was where most journalists aspired to go when their apprenticeship was served. But there was the bitter-sweet knowledge, even as we scanned the jobs pages of the *Press Gazette*, that we'd probably never again enjoy the same freedom to pursue our craft honestly that we had on a good local paper.

Jo Bannister today.

borrowed from British libraries. Various of her books and short stories have been translated into French, German, Italian, Danish, Swedish, Czech, Polish and Japanese.

Michael Wolsey
...remembers

Spectator picture.

AFTER leaving the *Spectator* Michael Wolsey worked for Recorder Newspapers in the East End of London. He was later foreign editor of the *Liverpool Daily Post*, features editor and then night editor of the *Irish Press*, Dublin, and, subsequently, deputy editor of the *Irish Independent*, Dublin.

He is now director of Ceannline, a media consultancy company which specialises in the editing and design of newspapers and magazines. He is married with three adult children and lives in Bettystown, Co Meath.

IN 1968 a legend walked back through the gates of Clandeboye Park. Charlie Tully had suffered a few acrimonious months as manager of Bangor Football Club four years earlier. Perhaps it was his odd sense of humour that persuaded the Clown Prince of Soccer to have another go at running the Irish League's least successful team.

He had better luck this time and in 1970 ended Bangor's unenviable record as the only league club never to have won a senior trophy. The Glasgow Celtic hero achieved this, in part, by establishing a link with his old club, which sent a number of young players his way on the Tully nursery programme. At the other end of the age scale, Tully also persuaded a few old Celtic warriors to tog out in yellow and blue, adding a distinctly green tinge to the Bangor colours.

Not surprisingly, this drew some barbed comments from visiting supporters, particularly the boys from Windsor Park. There were jibes about Celtic Reserves and yellow always being the right colour for Parkhead paddies. Harmless stuff.

But from my elevated perch in the Clandeboye Park press box – one phone, three seats – I began to observe a nastier edge creeping in. Sectarian insults were being slung Bangor's way, some of them pretty vicious. And this nasty stuff wasn't all coming from visitors. The worst of it came from a local gang who turned up every second week; not Bangor supporters but certainly people who lived in Bangor.

There was trouble outside the ground after one match. A bunch of these hoods had surrounded a few young Bangor fans. Fists and feet were flying along with sectarian abuse. Police intervention prevented what could have been a serious incident.

On the grand scale of football hooliganism, or Ulster sectarianism, it was minor stuff – shocking only because this was Bangor, and that sort of thing did not happen in Bangor. In the Sixties the town was a wonderful place for a young man to live and a young reporter to work; lively, quirky, liberal and tolerant. Its relative affluence and lack of sectarian division protected it from what passed for normality in most of Northern Ireland.

But by the end of the decade reality was knocking at the door. And reality was Civil Rights marches, clashes with police, a growing intolerance and evil men planning dark deeds.

The 1969 Stormont election was a bruising affair in Bangor, with an unofficial unionist, who backed Prime Minister Terence O'Neill, running against the party's choice, an anti-O'Neill candidate. The *Spectator* threw its editorial weight behind the (ultimately successful) O'Neill man and this brought some vitriol the way of its reporters.

Mostly it was harmless slagging. Some of it went further. I received threatening phone calls. At one public rally I was spat at. There were other straws in the wind. Offensive slogans daubed on the wall of a Catholic church; violence at an outdoor political meeting.

It was nothing, really. Most towns should have been so lucky. But this wasn't most towns. Reality was knocking at Bangor's door. Soon it would be inside and trampling around the place in muddy, steel-capped boots.

Michael Wolsey today.

THE *County Down Spectator* also witnessed faithful service during the late 1950s and into 1960 from Maureen Martin (now Mrs Jamison) and, during the mid to late 1960s, from Jack Ledgerwood, whose shorthand skills saw him rise to the position of senior editor with *Hansard* in London. Sadly, he passed away during the 1980s. This section of "Bangor in the Sixties" is respectfully dedicated to both Maureen and Jack.

Terence Bowman
...remembers

Bangor Boy

TO a child growing up in Bangor the Sixties stretched out like a vast adventure playground. Looking back now some 50 years, the decade began for me at the age of three when my parents, Hugh and Jean, my older brother Geoffrey, and I moved in the autumn of 1960 from a semi-detached house at 56 Thornleigh Gardens, right beside country lanes and open fields – long before the ring road was built – to 22 Waverley Drive.

Farewell to Thornleigh Gardens in 1960. Neighbourhood children are (back row, from left): Elizabeth McCarter, Elizabeth Clegg, Maurice Nesbitt, Terence Bowman. Back row: Geoffrey Bowman, Paul Tweed, Christine Clegg and John McCarter.

Our new home, which was detached, was built during the First World War. It came with an ancient gas oven, a heavy black Bakelite telephone complete with pull-out drawer to note down a dozen important numbers, a hideaway under the stairs, an extra toilet outside in the yard and a giant water butt at the side of the house that was used for collecting rain water. There were gas lights on the street and men in vans would arrive at our front door each week to deliver fish, milk and bread.

Not only did we have a large back garden lined with

My first visit to Ballyholme – with mother Jean and older brother Geoffrey.

Favourite shops for Bangor housewives in the pre-supermarket era – Furey's (above) and Smyth and McClure's, both pictured in 1962.

tall trees that could be climbed, but Ballyholme Beach was at the bottom of our road. My day-to-day world may have been confined to an area within a few hundred yards of the house, but it didn't matter. Boredom was a concept my generation never encountered, for like Doctor Who's Tardis, our playground was much larger on the inside that it appeared from the outside and there was never enough time for everything we wanted to do.

It was an era when the nearest thing to a mobile 'phone was two tin cans connected by a length of string and a public telephone still carried instructions to push buttons A and B. It was also a time when an already busy mother shopped each day, from Monday to Friday, and she usually had to take her children with her until they were ready for school.

By the dawn of the Sixties, my brother was already attending the PNEU (Parents' National Education Union) school at Farnham Park, so my mother was in the fortunate position of having just one child to care for during term time. With my fare costing a penny, we would catch the bus from the Groomsport Road and travel into the town centre.

Without a car, my mother's shopping list depended largely on what she could carry. She bought groceries between three well-known businesses on Main Street – the charmingly old-fashioned Millsopp's Stores, Hugh Furey's and Smyth and McClure's. The latter for quite a few years was the nearest thing Bangor had to a supermarket, with an extensive selection of goods displayed on two floors.

Her sole destination each Wednesday was the market, where she was able to buy fresh fruit and vegetables, as well as assorted household goods from the various stalls. Although today it's almost the stuff of mythology, there really was an elderly man who turned up from time to time to play the saw with a violin bow.

Dad Hugh relaxes with us on the beach – still wearing his business suit!

The main store for clothes was Simon's, close to the *Spectator* office on upper Main Street. It was Bangor's answer to the Grace Brothers department store in *Are You Being Served?* Packages were wrapped in brown paper and kept secure with string tied in a bow. There was a pneumatic tube system that sent money and messages to the offices with a "whoosh." The loss of Simon's in a major fire was a blow from which the town centre never really recovered.

The 'hut' at Ward Park, home for some four years in the early to mid-Sixties to the Connor House P2 class – it has survived to tell the tale.

When it was time for me to go to school, aged five years and one month – there was no playgroup, reception or infants' class – Connor House was the automatic choice. My father had attended Bangor Grammar School and its predecessor, the Endowed School, while my brother was already in P3.

'FIRST' DANCE CLUB
present
BOXING-NITE
AT THE DUCKPOND
Balloons, Squeakers, Streamers
provided
8—11.59 p.m.

I was admitted without an interview and attended my first day at school in the 'hut' at Ward Park on Wednesday 25 April 1962. During the Sixties the premises had many other uses – as a Scout hall, as a venue for the young people's Duckpond music venue, and a dance hall for adults. Indeed, I used to arrive home convinced the diamonds I'd found on the floor were real, rather than from a dancer's glittering costume.

Ward Park was ideal for a school because it offered plenty of opportunities for nature study outings, with the added bonus of the wildlife pens and roaming ducks and geese in such close proximity. Art included drawing the Belfast-built and then newly launched SS *Canberra*, while the other lessons were interspersed with such innovations as 'musical movement,' which was broadcast from a large radio mounted on the wall.

My first day at school – 25 April 1962. Geoffrey was already in P3.

After a year there, during which our efforts in the classroom were acknowledged with coloured stars in our exercise books, we didn't have to move too far as the main Connor House was located within the car park at the Tonic Cinema. The building had previously served as the clubhouse for Bangor Golf Club and was clearly nearing the end of its useful life. Being educated there, in relatively primitive conditions, ensured we respected the new school at Clifton Road when it finally opened its doors at the beginning of 1966. We had to wear black 'gutties' to protect the new floors and we definitely never ran in the corridors!

'This might hurt a little...'

ILLNESS and inoculations were very much a way of life for a child growing up in the early 1960s. Mumps, chicken pox and the measles were taken for granted and would be factored into the school year. Very few children didn't face a couple of weeks in bed while battling one of the era's contagious diseases, against which there was no routine inoculation.

Waking up with a sore throat was every child's nightmare for it often pointed to a spell in hospital, the swift removal of the tonsils and the consolation of a diet of jelly and ice-cream. It was usually a case of 'take out the tonsils first and ask questions later.'

There was the occasional visit to Dr Dick Roxburgh's clinic on Central Avenue to be inoculated against diseases like smallpox, diphtheria or polio. We just missed out on the polio vaccine in a lump of sugar, instead having to endure what seemed like an exceptionally large needle. We were told how important it was to be inoculated against polio in particular. In truth, there were few people, including children at school, who didn't know some unfortunate adult or youngster who had to struggle along the street or from classroom to classroom wearing callipers or using crutches.

The first time I needed hospital treatment occurred in the summer of 1962 when I was five and enjoying my first school holidays. I was playing football in our neighbours' garden with a group of boys, some as old as 11 or 12. Suddenly I was pushed boisterously to the ground – by my own brother. As the game continued around me I realised my left hand and arm to the

elbow were somewhat askew. Tears flowed and, as was the way in those times, the doctor was called. Our GP was Dr James Browne, whose surgery was on Hamilton Road, close to the New Savoy Hotel.

It wasn't long before he arrived at the house and diagnosed the problem; I'd dislocated my wrist. I had visions of a plaster cast – in fact, I *wanted* a plaster cast to show off to my friends. However, he applied a heavy bandage and used a stiff cardboard box to protect the injured wrist pending a visit to Newtownards Hospital the following day. There the duty doctor, after warning me that "this might hurt for a moment," gave my arm a sharp twist and the bones slipped back into place. More tears flowed, but that was it. No more pain and, to my continuing disappointment, no plaster cast or other proof I'd been injured.

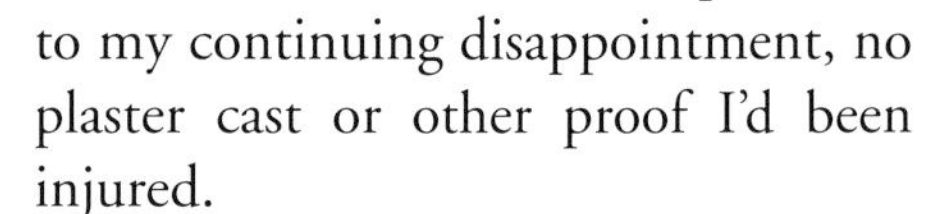

Having managed to avoid the dreaded tonsillectomy, I did, however, fall foul of its near relative, the adenoidectomy, in mid-November 1964. At the age of seven I was away from home, and family, for the first time. The surgery was carried out at Bangor Hospital during a three-day stay in a private room. My parents and brother were frequent visitors – the latter eager to tell me I'd missed his birthday treat, a trip to the Tonic to see *Goldfinger* – but the nights were painfully lonely. Thankfully there was one familiar face, Mrs Thomson, wife of Connor House headmaster Gordon Thomson, who was on the nursing team.

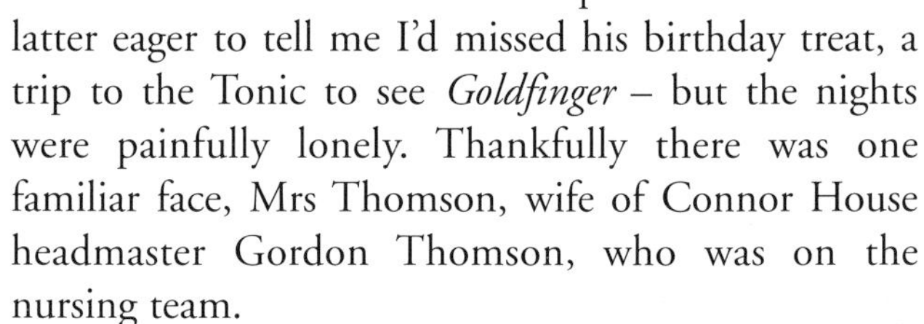

When the time came for my operation – to remove small lumps of tissue similar to the tonsils where the throat meets the back of the nose – I was given a pinky-coloured liquid to drink. Then came the injection to put me 'under.' I was told to count from 10 down to one, but all I can remember was losing consciousness with the theme tune to *The Man From*

Uncle reverberating around my head.

Within a week I was back at school, fully recovered but with little to show for my experience. Those who'd already gone under the knife to have their tonsils removed felt my visit to hospital "just to have my adenoids out" wasn't the same rite of passage they'd endured.

I had to wait another two years before I could claim some sort of fame, for an injury sustained while serving as one of Robin Hood's merry men. With a long garden at the back of our house, there was plenty of room to set up targets for the bows and arrows we made using bamboo canes, rocket sticks and lengths of string. The end result wasn't exactly banana-shaped but there was still sufficient tautness to send a rocket stick arrow a considerable distance.

On this summer's afternoon a school friend and I were recreating a battle with the Sheriff of Nottingham's soldiers when one of his 'arrows' flew straight at me and hit me on the face, about two inches from my right eye. It seemed a straightforward enough injury. Thankful I hadn't been blinded, my mother took me to the doctor's surgery where I had the obligatory tetanus injection. That should have been that, except the wound refused to heal and my right cheek began to swell up very noticeably.

With the problem still persisting after about a week, Dr Browne decided there was no alternative but to have me admitted to the hospital for an exploratory operation. It involved another three-day stay in the same private room, another missed film at the Tonic, yet more of the pinky medicine and a reprise of *The Man From Uncle* theme.

The surgery produced an inch-long piece of wood that had somehow become separated from the arrow and lodged itself deep in my cheek. Once it was removed and the infection was treated, the swelling started to go down, although I was left with a noticeable scar that impressed my friends. My mother kept the piece of wood in a plastic box as a warning that the back garden wasn't Sherwood Forest and bows and arrows shouldn't be pointed at anyone.

The early months of 1963 certainly experienced "a decent fall of snow."

The Four Seasons

DURING the Sixties the sun really did shine every summer for weeks on end and no winter would have been complete without a decent fall of snow. The proof can be found in the pages of the *County Down Spectator*, with pictures galore of children enjoying themselves at Pickie Pool or Ballyholme Beach during July and August, and then, months later, grabbing a tea tray from the kitchen to hurtle down the snow-covered hill at Kingsland.

All year round there was never enough time in the day and boredom was a word that hadn't been invented. Having fun rarely involved anything with a power source, the special exception being the Scalextric set your Dad bought at Christmas, but which never quite lived up to the thrill-packed experience promised in the commercials.

School dominated term-time weekdays, but weekends were always full of promise. Even if the heavens opened up, inviting sanctuary could always be found at the Carnegie Library on Hamilton Road. If you arrived from Moira Drive you could hop, skip and jump your way down the steps that emerged close to the children's playground, which featured more than a few modern-day death traps. Few could resist trying to defy gravity on the maypole. Then it was a quick dash round to the front of the library, in through the double doors and straight to the children's section on the right. If you were really lucky and no one was ahead of you, that week's copies of *The Beano* and *The Dandy*, the only two comics the library stocked, would be on the rack. Being able to read them there meant you could get something else at home, like *The Topper* or *The Beezer*, which your older brother would read even if he supposedly preferred the *Eagle*, *Boys' World* or *The Hornet*.

Children enjoying the maypole and swings in Ward Park on Wednesday, oblivious of the lively debate which took place on this subject at the previous nig ht's meeting of Banger Borough Council.
'Spectator' Photo. 36/35/1.

We all enjoyed reading, with Enid Blyton's *Secret Seven* and *Famous Five* mystery stories, along with Hergé's *Tintin* books, being among our favourites. It was always a special occasion when a new story arrived on the shelves.

Ward Park was always popular after a visit to the library and most boys sailed wooden boats in the adjacent pond. Chasing after your vessel to the other side could have been done by the path over the flat bridge, but many of us preferred the more hazardous route across the fast-flowing weir, which park caretaker Frank Russell told us led all the way down to the seafront at Queen's Parade. Just as well there was a wire guard over the tunnel to prevent small boats and little boys from discovering whether the story was true.

After hanging upside down on the First World War gun till the blood rushed to your head and then attempting to blow the spire off Hamilton Road Presbyterian Church by turning some of the handles, it was on to see the birds of various shapes and sizes that were kept in cages and pens, or roamed freely around the upper ponds. The peacocks with their magnificent tail feathers were visitors' favourites, but nothing matched the appeal of the vast rabbit compound, which was dotted with little houses into which the rabbits scuttled when they weren't out greeting the public in exchange for a few blades of grass. The only way to gain access to the compound was by boat, from the far side. I became the envy of my class at school after Billy Ward, Mr Russell's successor, rowed me over to select a new pet rabbit after the death of its predecessor.

Park Drive – with the old fountain just out of view – during the work in the early 1960s to create the familiar parking bays. *Spectator* picture.

If you were feeling thirsty the answer lay at the nearby bowling green, where senior citizens rolled heavy balls from one end to the other and then back again. It was at the Park Drive side that one found the iron drinking fountain. If you pushed the penny-sized brass button, out flowed cold, satisfying water. There were several more fountains around the town, including a particularly ornate one at the McKee Clock. Both locations had putting greens, as did Kingsland, where there was also a more expensive pitch and putt course on the lower and upper levels.

The Tonic Cinema in 1962, when it was hosting Imperial Bowls as an added attraction.

A few hundred yards from Ward Park was another place where we spent many happy hours, especially on Saturday afternoons. The Tonic Cinema ran continuous programmes, which meant if you missed the start of a film you just sat on for the next screening. By the early Sixties Bangor had two remaining cinemas, the Tonic and the Queen's, but the latter had something of a reputation so trips there were rare and certainly never in the evening. To reach the kiosk and cinema you followed the long alleyway off Queen's

Parade, passing posters that advertised forthcoming attractions. There was *always* a poster for a Godzilla film and another for one of the Dracula series starring Christopher Lee.

My first film, in late 1961, was Walt Disney's *The Swiss Family Robinson*, followed by *Jason and the Argonauts*, with its stop-motion wizardry that brought sword-wielding skeletons to life. In between those two films, the family tried out the new Imperial Bowls that had been installed in the former restaurant. It was my first experience of bowling and for many years afterwards I was convinced it had been a real 10-pin bowling alley, rather than a short-lived arcade-style game with flashing lights.

The Beatles' films *A Hard Day's Night* and *Help!*, anything involving James Bond, John Wayne or Kirk Douglas, along with *Mary Poppins* and *The Sound of Music*, all attracted huge attendances, adults included, with queues often stretching in both directions – towards the New Savoy Hotel at the Hamilton Road roundabout, and round the back of the cinema almost as far as Broadway.

Before seeing your favourite film, you could buy sweets inside the cinema but the choice was limited, whereas the Sweet Shop (previously Peter Pan) outside, on the far right of the building, had countless jars of assorted favourites that would last the afternoon and could be bought in two or four-ounce measures. Particularly popular on a chilly day were the hot roasted peanuts, sold from a yellow-stained glass container that sat on the counter.

Once inside the cinema, the upstairs circle, although a little dearer, was always best, and safest. You just never knew when something was going to land on your head if you were down below in the stalls. Indeed, sometimes you didn't want to know what that

something was!

During the intermission a choc ice from the usherette's tray, dimly illuminated by a tiny electric bulb as she walked down the aisles, was an absolute must – but you had to be quick or you would be stuck with a plain tub of Bangor Maid ice cream, which you had to dig into with a little wooden spoon.

Films bore one of the three certifications in the Sixties: U (universal), A (children had to be accompanied by an adult) and X (you had to be over 16). I was too young to see an X-film during the Sixties, but that didn't mean I didn't know they existed. There was always someone at school who would claim he'd managed to sneak into the Queen's to see *Helga*, which rather than the orgy of sexual depravity everyone assumed it was, proved to be a German sex education film. Another much talked-about film, *Karamojo*, was also screened at the Queen's in the Sixties. Recommended for "mature adult viewing," the posters boasted "blood-chilling acts that can never be filmed again" and "teenage maidens in a pre-marriage ritual." In fact it was an hour-long natural history documentary from the 1950s.

The posters you passed on the way upstairs in the Tonic, not to mention the alleyway at the Queen's, played a part in any Bangor boy's early sex education. One of the most striking images was for the erotic science fiction film *Barbarella*, starring Jane Fonda. Another was for *The Graduate*, X-rated then yet very tame by modern standards.

To cool down the best place was the sea at Ballyholme, or the stretch of beach at Queen's Parade. Ballyholme, nowadays largely deserted by swimmers, was packed during the summer holidays. The raft moored a short distance out was

A packed Ballyholme beach on Tuesday 4 August 1964 – hottest day of the year in Northern Ireland. *Spectator* picture.

for anyone who couldn't swim but wanted to feel they were doing something a little daring. However, with the tide full in the wooden diving platforms were only for the bravest.

If you lived close to the beach there was no need to pay for a bathing box. You just wore your costume under your clothes, grabbed a towel and raced down to the shore, where you stripped and dashed into the water, hoping it wasn't too cold. After a swim you did an intricate Houdini-style manoeuvre underneath the towel and emerged once again fully clothed.

Making the most of the good weather at Ballyholme.
"Spectator" Photo.

Clutching the last pennies of your pocket money you had a couple of choices without needing to go too far: either the beach shop just past the bathing boxes, or Seabreeze, the big red-

'Seabreeze' opposite Waverley Drive – which proved very popular on a hot summer day (of which there were many).

bricked house opposite Waverley Drive, which could be reached directly from the promenade. Both carried an extensive selection of iced lollies, but Seabreeze was everyone's favourite; it was as if there was something different about their refrigeration system that gave the lollies a distinctive taste and texture.

The beach shop made a particularly fine ice cream slider or you could buy a packet of wafers for 2d and eat them as a substitute for biscuits. If you'd no money at all, it didn't matter as the same shop redeemed empty Coca Cola and the newly-launched Fanta bottles for cash and didn't ask where you'd got them (Fanta having replaced Sukie SunKap orange juice in our affections). A quick look around the beach would do the trick. Indeed, if you were prepared to search as far as the Seacliff Road or in the opposite direction to Ballymacormick Point, you could easily make half-a-crown in an afternoon. It was an early example of recycling.

SunKap at Breakfast
REGD. TRADE MARK
freshens you up for the day!
Start the day really refreshed with orange Sunkap! It's made from whole fresh oranges- that's why the family love it. Order Sunkap daily from your milkman.
SuKie
SunKap
ORANGE DRINK
Made from wHole fresH oranges
Sukie
Get SunKap every morning from your milkman

Fanta replaced Sukie SunKap orange juice in our affections.

Children who attended the CSSM at Ballyholme Beach in July 1964. *Spectator* picture.

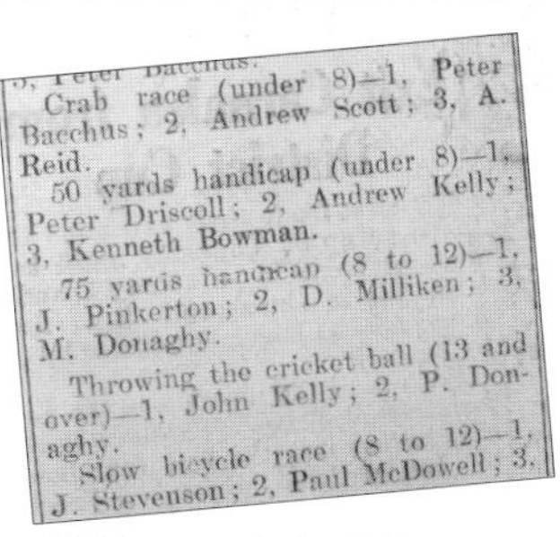
Crab race (under 8)—1, Peter Bacchus; 2, Andrew Scott; 3, A. Reid.
50 yards handicap (under 8)—1, Peter Driscoll; 2, Andrew Kelly; 3, Kenneth Bowman.
75 yards handicap (8 to 12)—1, J. Pinkerton; 2, D. Milliken; 3, M. Donaghy.
Throwing the cricket ball (13 and over)—1, John Kelly; 2, P. Donaghy.
Slow bicycle race (8 to 12)—1, J. Stevenson; 2, Paul McDowell; 3.

CSSM sports day in 1964 – Kenneth (that's Terence) Bowman shares the honours with Dick Milliken!

Also very popular during the summer months, especially with parents, was the Children's Special Service Mission – the CSSM – at Ballyholme Park. Although essentially of a religious nature, to the children attending, some as young as five or six, the meetings were a great opportunity for organised fun and games with friends and neighbours. After a variety of largely beach-based competitions, including tide fights, scavenger hunts and sand-designing contests, the climax was the sports day in Ward Park, featuring such challenges as the bunny hop (for girls), the crab race (for boys) and the legendary slow bicycle race.

The first time my name appeared in the *Spectator* was in 1963, when I finished third in the CSSM's 50-yard race (under eight), the winner being my friend and neighbour Peter Driscoll. Unfortunately, my name was recorded on the results sheet as 'Kenneth', rather than Terence. The report did, however show, in the next line, that the runner-up over 75 yards (eight to 12 years) was future Ulster, Ireland and Lions rugby hero Dick Milliken. It was the first and last time our names appeared together in a sports report!

However, no summer was complete without a season ticket for Pickie Pool. If you couldn't swim there was no better place to learn, under the watchful eye of

Taking part in a mid-1960s CSSM tide fight at Ballyholme Beach: the Bowman brothers with Gilbert Nesbitt and John Adrain. Also in view is Richard Hogg, while Gilbert's mother Dorrie is at the back with the cine camera.

This Milk Marketing Board-sponsored sand designing competition from the early 1960s was held on the stretch of beach at Queen's Parade. The judges were Miss Marjorie Mason (left) and Mrs Morrison, manageress of the Mimba milk bar and the winning entry, showing Yogi Bear, was designed by Robert Crangle, Michael Burch, Paul Rea and Ronald Crangle.
Spectator picture.

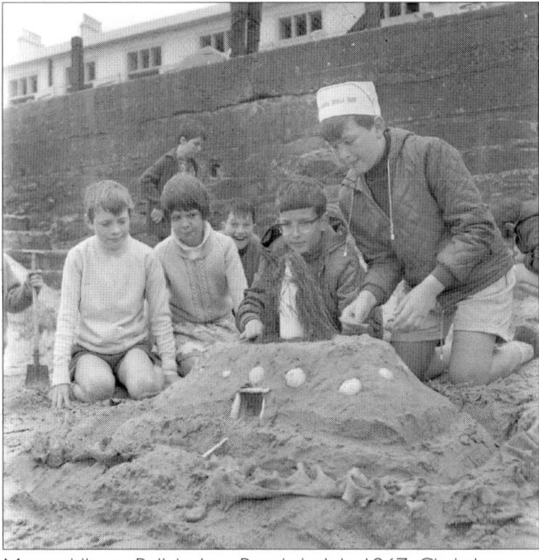

Meanwhile, at Ballyholme Beach in July 1967, Christine Wellwood (left) and Rosemary Brookes admire the sand-designing talents of David Higginbotham and Paul Tweed.
Spectator picture.

'Uncle Andy' Johnston. He had been a permanent fixture there from the 1920s, teaching the fathers and grandfathers of the children who queued up to be tethered to the length of rope he used to gently pull the budding swimmer through the water at the special learners' corner.

More often than not, the water was cold but not numbingly so. The temperature in Fahrenheit was chalked on a board that greeted swimmers arriving at the pool and if it was over 60 degrees then that was bearable. It was certainly much warmer than the outdoor area of open sea water with its accompanying raft that could in theory only be reached from inside Pickie. Not quite, for it offered free entry to Pickie for those daring swimmers who didn't mind arriving without their clothes.

While the autumn brought with it the disappointment of going back to school, it meant Hallowe'en was drawing ever nearer. "Just make sure you don't throw them at anyone" was about as far as the safety lessons went in those days, yet few of us knew anyone who'd been injured by a carelessly thrown or discarded firework.

Hallowe'en was always a family-orientated occasion with neighbours organising parties on successive nights so children could visit each one in turn, enjoy the fun and games and then the fireworks in the back garden. There was no finer tradition than dunking for apples in a bucket of water, while the Hallowe'en fayre included a barmbrack containing a ring, which most certainly wasn't made from gold, and an apple tart with a silver threepenny bit hidden in the filling.

Our school would also join in the Hallowe'en festivities, with a huge fireworks display at College Avenue following a trip away from Bangor and a meal in the canteen on our return. Each class year had a different destination, including Bellevue Zoo, the fire station at Ormeau Avenue, the Ormeau Bakery, and the old Transport Museum, all in Belfast, as well as the Silent Valley reservoir in the Mournes.

The final stretch of the year moved painfully slowly, enlivened occasionally by an early fall of snow, but it was worth the wait. The beginning of December was early enough for me to start ticking the days off the calendar and then, within about a week of Christmas, the hours as well. Lessons would be abandoned for the run-in to the holiday break and we would be allowed to play games or bring in a favourite toy. Strips of coloured paper would be converted into paper chains which we would hang from the windows, along with other Christmas decorations.

Although the new Co-Op at the bottom of Main Street had its own in-store Santa, he could not compete with the thrill of going to Belfast to see the enormous Christmas tree and sparkling illuminations at the City Hall and then visiting the "real" Father Christmas in Robb's at Castle Place. We would either journey by car to the outskirts of the city and then travel the rest of the way on a trolleybus, or we would catch the train at Bangor station – pausing to use the nameplate machine to punch out our names on aluminium strips for sixpence – and then walk from Queen's Quay into the city centre.

Seeing Santa in his special grotto was a major highlight of the Christmas holidays because it usually meant a trip in a spaceship or a magic carriage. Whatever the mode of transport, you could be sure of one thing – the sense of motion would be very realistic thanks, no doubt, to a few hefty men giving the stationary vehicle a serious shaking!

By the mid-1960s, when the secret of Santa was finally out in our household, there was no question of cancelling the trip to the city. Tapping into the popularity enjoyed by the BBC's *Doctor Who*, Santa was replaced for one Christmas only by a giant Dalek dispensing the gifts while threatening to "exterrrrminate" us – an experience we wouldn't have missed for the world.

As far as family presents were concerned, my brother and I would make our seasonal visit to the Belfast Savings Bank at upper Main Street, where Liam Tweed would personally handle our withdrawals. A single pound note each, accumulated from cash gifts received during the year, was enough for four presents with a little left over to buy ourselves something in Mark's toy shop. My Dad had his account close by, at the Belfast Banking Company (soon to be amalgamated with the Northern Bank), where the most familiar face was that of Norman Douglas, later to serve as branch manager. An RNLI charity box sat on the counter and if you

The ever-popular Woolworth's store at the bottom of Main Street.

STEWART Miller, although more known now for its range of toys and confectionery, was originally established as a Bookseller and Stationer in Bangor in the early 1950s, first on the corner of Main Street and King Street (now the Clarks shoe shop), and later down the street in premises adjacent to the existing TK Maxx store (subsequently destroyed in a terrorist attack).

Over the years the name has been a familiar one on Bangor's Main Street, having, at various times, occupied five different sites, including Warden's Corner (Boots Corner) and upper Main Street, as well as lower Main Street. In addition, the company operated a large branch at the Clandeboye Shopping Centre, which was destroyed by fire in July 1987.

The company still maintains a sizeable presence in the town, at the Flagship Centre, and also operates in the neighbouring towns of Newtownards and Holywood.

pushed the lifeboat into the boathouse, then dropped a penny into the slot the bright red vessel would shoot back with a terrific clatter before swallowing your donation. It was definitely worth the sacrifice!

As for that single pound note, its Sixties purchasing power would ensure beaming smiles all round on Christmas morning – for my Dad, a tin of Henri Wintermans miniature cigars I'd bought on my own in Gardiners; for my grandmother, a packet of scented bath cubes from Balmers; for my brother, a Dan Dare pencil case from Stewart Miller or a balsa wood glider from McCulloughs down on Bridge Street, and for Mum, it was back up to Woolworths for a dress ring with a sparkling red stone.

The strange thing about the ring was that, although my mother would show it off with obvious pride as she and my Dad set off for a New Year's Eve party, it never featured in any of the pictures taken of the revellers when the clock struck midnight!

... *and at Number One it's Cecil Greenwood!*

CHILDREN growing up in Bangor in the 1960s always had their favourite shops. Not the ones their mothers dragged them along to every time they needed a new pair of shoes or trousers or a haircut, but the special ones that left a lasting impression.

In time-honoured fashion here, in reverse order with one high climber, are the Top Five businesses Bangor youngsters loved to visit, with or without their parents' approval!

The Co-Op's Norman Keenan in 1965 behind Van Morrison (front, third from right) with members of The Falcons at the Andrews' Memorial Hall in Comber, and below. Special thanks to Norman Keenan and Harry Filmer, also to James G. Meredith and Derek Beattie.

High climber: The Co-Op at the bottom of Main Street. This place, after it opened in May 1964, immediately gave long-time favourite Woolworth's a run for its money and replaced Mitchell's, which moved from Hamilton Road to upper Main Street, as the best place to buy chart hits and LPs. The ground floor record department, managed by Norman Keenan, a man with a great love for music and a keen involvement in the local music scene, was vast. It also featured small booths where a potential buyer could hear a track or two before making the commitment to spent nearly £2 on a new album.

The Co-Op also had moving escalators, ideal for dashing down the one that was moving up or vice versa, and a pedoscope in the footwear department upstairs that purportedly showed you an X-ray of each foot to ensure your new shoes would fit properly. There was the Tartan Room cafe with windows overlooking Main Street where you could be left with crayons and a colouring-in book, and at Christmas the place was a blaze of colour with Santa's Wonderland taking centre stage.

5. **Templeton's** (104 Abbey Street). You would happily have walked all the way from Ballyholme to Andy Templeton's for he seemed to sell more varieties of sweets than any other shop in the town. Not only did he stock rock-hard penny gobstoppers, but he also sold lumps of a yellow rock-like material which, if you were lucky, after biting your way through it, might contain a real coin. One can only begin to imagine the modern-day Health and Safety regulations that such items of confectionery would have breached.

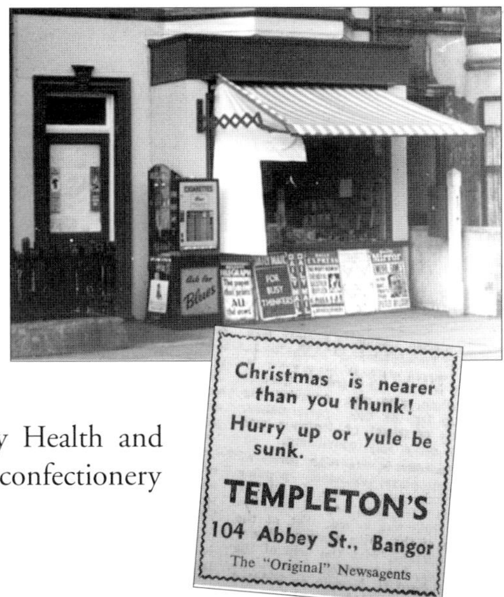

4. **Kannenberg's/ formerly H. E. North** (126 High Street, near Prospect Road junction). For children attending Connor House, once it moved to Clifton Road, and Bangor Grammar School, this was the handiest shop at break or lunchtime. It was one of the first places in the town to declare that no more than three children could be on the premises at the same time. Little wonder too, for at times it seemed as if there were more youngsters in the long, narrow shop than in the playground.

3. **Mark's Toy Shop** (1 Central Avenue). Nowhere came even close to Mark's at Christmas or birthday time since the shelves of nearest rival Woolworth's tended to be stacked high with mass-produced plastic toys that offered little excitement to the would-be cowboy, secret agent or garage owner. Mark's, on the other

NO PARKING PROBLEMS
SHOP IN COMFORT at
L. K. MARK & CO.
84 MAIN STREET : BANGOR
Large Display of
MODERN TOYS including TRI-ANG, HORNBY, MECCANO, LEGO, SCALEXTRIC, KIDDICRAFT, SUNBEAM and MOBO TOYS
OPEN FRIDAY NIGHTS UNTIL 9 p.m.

hand, was a veritable Aladdin's Cave of toys and games, from bags of marbles, model cars and plastic soldiers to board games like Monopoly and Risk, as well as Meccano and Lego.

Barry's Amusements – a favourite destination for children of all ages.

2. Amusement arcades (18-20 Quay Street, 10 Quay Street, 4 Queen's Parade and Queen's Arcade). There was no shortage of 'fun centres' along the seafront, with Barry's, the Palladium, the Winter Gardens and former Councillor George Allport's premises further along Queen's Parade open virtually all the year round. Barry's was an indoor fairground with "for amusement only" games, ancient fruit machines, the ghost train, dodgem cars, a laughing policeman and a fortune teller whose predictions appeared on a printed card, not to mention the helter-skelter that stretched high into the sky.

You didn't really go there with the idea of winning money; rather to witness a slice of life from a bygone era. Who could ever forget the penny-in-the-slot machines on the way into Barry's that recreated scenes like a public hanging or an execution by guillotine with little moving figures acting out the parts? During the summer months Barry's also operated an outdoor amusement park on the small pier on the opposite side of the road, with swing-boats, a merry-go-round and a rollercoaster.

Both the Palladium and the Winter Gardens were more renowned for their gaming machines with plenty of flashing lights, although no one was ever likely to make a fortune with a prize limit of just a shilling. All the same, that last penny in your pocket or the one lying unclaimed in one of the slots could go a long way if you were fortunate enough to notch up three bells on the fruit machine, place it clear of the lines on the roll-a-penny machine, or position it perfectly to push a stack of pennies into your eagerly awaiting hands.

Picture courtesy of John Scully and www.bangorlocal.com

The Queen's Arcade amusements were a cross between Barry's and the Palladium, with pennies to be won on horse-racing machines that carried the names of top jockeys like Scobie Breasley, Pat Taaffe and Lester Piggott, or other games of chance that featured stars of the silver screen like Jean Harlow, Bette Davis and Marlene Dietrich. The secret to its survival lay in the fact it was the nearest arcade to Pickie Pool and had its own candyfloss machine.

1. Cecil Greenwood (54 High Street). No shop meant more to little boys in Bangor, not to mention countless hundreds of holidaymakers, than Cecil's cramped store that stretched back forever and sold just about everything from rude seaside postcards to stink bombs, tricks and jokes. To the authorities running the town, Cecil Greenwood's shop was something of an embarrassment, but in truth there were few men in Bangor who hadn't visited it for one reason or

Mayne's garage at Main Street. Picture and information courtesy of Jim Mayne.

another at some time in their lives.

It was also the only shop in Bangor that sold a wide selection of American comics. Without Cecil Greenwood, many Bangor children would never have known about *Mad* magazine or superheroes like Batman, Superman, the Incredible Hulk and the Fantastic Four. Where else could you have bought a fake nail to stick through your finger, counterfeit money "to fool your friends" or a stick of chewing gum that snapped like a mousetrap when you pulled it from the pack?

Cecil Greenwood was never going to win any awards for Bangor Businessman of the Year, bearing in mind those *other* magazines that were purchased by the great and the good of the town for decades, but in his own unique way he did as much to maintain the town's position as a leading seaside resort during the early years of the Troubles as many others in the business community.

Honorary mentions: Wright's (Coronation) Cafe (1a Albert Street) for one of the best 99s in town; Mayne's (118 Main Street) and Marshall's (62-64 Abbey Street) for new and second-hand bicycles and cycle repairs; Robert Neill and Sons (137 Main Street) for the teddy bears in the window; Pollocks (29 Gray's Hill) for fishing nets on the way to Stricklands Glen; Isobel's (11-12 Queen's Parade) for having so many varieties of sweets in the window and for defying the developers long after other businesses had closed; the *Spectator* office (109 Main Street), where you could get your name spelt out backwards on lead type during a school visit, and the shop outside the railway station – but carefully avoiding the wasps that swarmed around the Coca Cola machine.

J. & R. Mayne's garage ran from 1924 until 1964, selling and repairing a wide range of bicycles. The firm also repaired cars and charged batteries. In those days many country radios also ran on batteries and these were charged on a weekly basis. There were usually 24 being charged at any one time. James Mayne died in 1961, with Robert continuing the business until 1964, when it was sold to Maxol and subsequently to Messrs P.W. (Walter) Gethin.

Me and my music

MY enduring love for Sixties pop music began at the dawn of the decade, thanks to my father and his investment in a record player so that he could relax after work while reading his paper and listening to classical music. A man still in his thirties, he bought the occasional pop record if he liked it, which was why my early musical education was given direction by two of skiffle king Lonnie Donegan's finest, "My Old Man's A Dustman" and "The Battle of New Orleans," plus a double A-sided disc which combined anonymously recorded versions of "Deck of Cards" and "Atlantis" (chart hits for Wink Martindale and The Shadows respectively).

All three records were played constantly, along with a bizarre 45rpm recording by American soprano Florence Foster Jenkins (who was to music what William McGonigall was to poetry), which showed my father had a sense of humour.

Meanwhile, in Liverpool the blue touch paper had been lit for the music revolution that would sweep all before it, including a six-year-old boy in Bangor. There were few opportunities to hear music at that tender age, other than *Children's Favourites* on a Saturday morning, where, gradually, records by The Beatles began to vie for attention beside Ronnie Hilton's "Windmill In Old Amsterdam" and "Sparky's Magic Piano" by Danny Kaye.

I was given a 6/8d record token by an aunt for Christmas 1963 and as soon as the shops reopened after the holidays I begged and cajoled my mother into taking me to Mitchell's, then located on Hamilton Road, where I quickly became the proud owner of my very first Beatles record, "I Want To Hold Your Hand." Within weeks I'd also acquired a copy

of "She Loves You," thus beginning a pattern which saw my collection growing every few months as the group released yet another chart-topping single.

With my three best friends from Waverley Drive we formed our own version of The Beatles, standing on tomato boxes complete with borrowed tennis rackets and a few dustbin lids. Since one of our group was a girl, she had to be Ringo while there was a constant battle between the rest of us over who got to be John or Paul, with George barely getting a look in.

When The Beatles appeared in Belfast in 1964 I envied the neighbouring teenagers whose parents allowed them to see their idols in the flesh. By way of compensation my mother took me to Bertie McConnell's shop on High Street. There I bought three packets of Beatles bubble gum cards. The pink square of chewing gum tasted strange compared to the usual mint flavour from the machine at the bottom of our road, but it meant I had nine different images of The Beatles to show off to my friends at school. Unlike *The Man from Uncle*, *Batman* and American Civil War cards I collected in later years, I never completed the set. Indeed, with 2d representing decent enough "sweet money" in those days (it was enough for eight Fruit Salads or eight Black Jacks), I never bought any more packs of Beatle cards, but those nine survived longer than anything that followed them.

By 1966, with the group spending much of their time in the studio, their music started to sound distinctly odd to my young ears. Thus my loyalty was tested with the arrival of an American rival on the scene. The Monkees not only performed catchy pop songs, but they were also very accessible – appearing on their own weekly television series. Davy Jones may have been English but Mickey Dolenz was the one we knew from his role in *Circus Boy.*

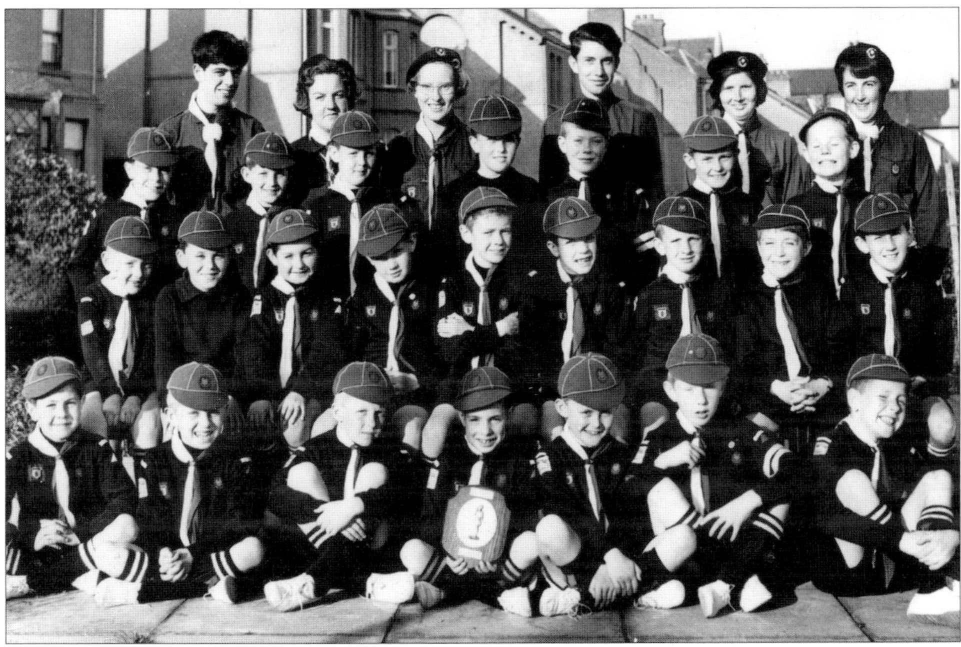

5th Bangor Cubs – occasional Beatles impersonators and winners of the Caswell Shield in 1967 for being the best Bangor pack at the County Flag competition. Back (from left): leaders Chris Wilson, Margaret Wilson, Betty McKee (Akela), Ivan Adair, Deirdre Adair, Maeve Garrett. Second row: Shane Wolsey, Martin Miller, Geoffrey Johnston, Bryan McGimpsey, Geoffrey Bowman, Richard Swanston, Richard Marshall. Third row: Stephen Miller, David Reid, Graham Neill, Ian Ferguson, Richard Smith, Peter Driscoll, William Hunter, Terence Bowman, Arnold Parkinson. Front row: Glyn Lawley, Ian Stewart, Patrick Ellison, Patrick McKee, Martin McMullan, Richard Hogg and Robert Mayne. *Spectator* picture.

Much as I really wanted to enjoy the music of The Beatles three years on, only a few of their songs had the same instant appeal as those early hits. One was "Yellow Submarine," which I sang with gusto in my one and only appearance in front of an audience. It was a 5th Bangor Cub Pack gang show in the hall at Springfield Avenue. Little did I realise it doubled as the 'Fo'c'sle' nightspot, which attracted real groups and real singers after we'd gone home.

My musical education, however, took a giant step forward thanks to the transistor radio I received for

BANGOR MEMORY - Laying cables in 1960 in preparation for the introduction of an automatic telephone service in Bangor. *Spectator* picture.

Christmas in December 1966. Until then the only radio in the house resembled a large wooden box with glowing valves and stations like Athlone, Budapest and Hilversum, as well as the BBC's Light Programme and Home Service, on its illuminated panel. While it could cope with Cliff Richard and The Beatles – but preferred *Listen With Mother* with Daphne Oxenford each weekday lunchtime – you could never imagine it playing the psychedelic sounds of Pink Floyd, Cream and Procul Harum.

Everything changed with the arrival of my own transistor radio, with a single earpiece which, within hours, had become permanently attached to the side of my head. This was especially the case at night, when I would drift off to sleep with the sounds of Radio Caroline North and Radio Luxembourg, or any foreign-language station still transmitting pop music, floating around in my head.

The radio would be on for hours on end, especially if I was ill in bed. The pirate stations that broadcast during the daytime gave way in time to the BBC's new Radio One. That I have always known so many songs from the Sixties, performed by an extensive range of artists, can only be explained by the subliminal impact of all those hours of listening to the radio, awake and asleep. And, of course, it helped to reawaken my love for the music of The Beatles.

I never arrived at school with a satchel crammed full of the latest gate-sleeved albums. Perhaps I was put off by our English teacher who decided to set aside part of a lesson one morning to analyse the lyrics of King Crimson's *In the Court of the Crimson King*. A track from the 1969 album included the opening lines:

Cat's foot iron claw
Neuro-surgeons scream for more

At paranoia's poison door
Twenty first century schizoid man.

He was none too impressed with what "prog rock" had to offer and suggested we would get more sense on the side of a cereal box. As for myself, I just knew what I liked and if I could see a group performing the song on *Top of the Pops*, then all the better.

My Sixties musical journey took me from "My Old Man's A Dustman," "She Loves You" and "A Hard Day's Night," past "Good Vibrations and "A Whiter Shade of Pale" to "I Heard It Through The Grapevine" and "Honky Tonk Women." I looked forward with eager anticipation to what the 1970s would offer. It was just a shame the first No 1 hit of the new decade was Rolf Harris's "Two Little Boys."

BANGOR MEMORY - Fifth Bangor Sea Scouts retained the County Challenge Flag in 1965. Front: P. Harvey, N. Clarke, M. Martin. Back: A. Ballantyne (Second), M. McConnell (Patrol Leader) and B. Harvey. *Spectator* picture.

My 1960s Top Thirty Singles

Barry Ryan – Eloise
Beach Boys – God Only Knows
Beatles – I Feel Fine
Beatles – Penny Lane
Bee Gees – First Of May
Billy J. Kramer And The Dakotas – Little Children
Bobby Goldsboro – Honey
Chris Montez – The More I See You
Cilla Black – Alfie
Dionne Warwick – Walk On By
Dusty Springfield – The Look Of Love
Elvis Presley – Suspicious Minds
Four Tops – Reach Out
Gary Puckett And The Union Gap –Young Girl
Gerry And The Pacemakers – Ferry 'Cross The Mersey
Glen Campbell – Wichita Lineman
Herb Alpert – This Guy's In Love With You

Hollies – He Ain't Heavy, He's My Brother
Ike And Tina Turner – River Deep and Mountain High
Keith West – Excerpt From A Teenage Opera
Mary Wells – My Guy
Monkees –Daydream Believer
Petula Clark – Downtown
Procul Harum – A Whiter Shade Of Pale
Righteous Brothers – You've Lost That Loving Feeling
Rolling Stones – Paint It Black
Scott Walker – Joanna
Simon Dupree and the Big Sound – Kites
Tom Jones – It's Not Unusual
Turtles – Happy Together

BANGOR MEMORY - Members of Bangor Parish Church choir sing carols at the town's Christmas tree in December 1961.

The Sunday treat

SUNDAY was different to any other day of the week for a child growing up in Bangor in the Sixties, even during the school holidays. It wasn't that our town was run by a puritan local authority which insisted – as happened elsewhere in Northern Ireland – that playground swings be chained up and we should spend the day reading the Bible. There was just an understanding that Sunday was not the day for making a racket on the street or kicking a ball around the garden.

My mother, whose own Presbyterian upbringing in the late 1920s and 1930s had been a strict one, exercised a more enlightened approach to matters of religion. Converting to the Church of Ireland in her late teens, she held the view that my brother and I should attend Sunday School and services at our local church, St Columbanus at Ballyholme, until we were teenagers, when we could make our own decisions about future attendance.

We learned considerably more at Sunday School

than we ever did during church services which, with all due respect to the Rev (later Canon) Jack Mercer, who had baptised me in 1957, were, to a young mind, largely repetitive, with prayers, hymns and the sermon followed by more hymns and more prayers. On the other hand, the Sunday School teachers, led by Eddie Beckett and Marsden Fitzsimons, rewarded us with stickers for our hymn books and, at the end of the year, prizes for progress in our Bible studies.

I can't imagine what our teacher must have thought when, on being asked what I would like for my efforts, I requested a large-scale model of *Thunderbird 2* on the basis that it was vastly superior to the two-inch version that came free with a packet of cereal!

Church services seemed endless and I would seek out new ways of making the time pass, from holding my breath for more than a minute to working out mathematical equations based on the hymn numbers displayed on a board above the pulpit. I would also leaf through the pages of the Book of Common Prayer to the section that showed the dates when Good Friday and Easter Monday would occur in the future. So while Mr Mercer was endeavouring to save my soul I was trying to work out if I would be in my 40s before my birthday next fell on Easter Sunday.

Sundays were far from dull and usually held out the promise of a family outing or a special treat. So long as it was dry, as a family we would always walk to See-Sea House on the Ballyholme Road to collect the Sunday papers. Our route would take us along the promenade and then through Ballyholme Park to the shop, where my brother and I would receive our weekly pocket money, which by the mid-Sixties amounted to a shilling. It was hard to resist the lure of shelves weighed down with children's favourites, including sweetie cigarettes and matches. The trick was to buy as many different things as

See-Sea House on the Ballyholme Road.

possible and make them last the rest of the day.

Once in a while my Dad, who had served in the RAF during the war, would treat us to an Airfix kit of a Spitfire or a Hurricane which we would assemble during the afternoon. There was always a great sense of satisfaction on completing the task and attaching the finished model to a piece of fishing line to show it in action.

Better still were the days we didn't have to attend church after Sunday School, for the extra time meant a walk to Caproni's and the promise of a 99 or anything else from the long list pinned to the wall.

My parents, Hugh and Jean Bowman, in the late 1960s.

Equally memorable for any young Bangorian was a visit to Stricklands Glen. The Glen – at Bangor West – covered a large expanse in the Sixties, with the surrounding open countryside rather than houses emphasising its role as an important area of recreational open space. Armed with fishing nets bought from Pollock's on Gray's Hill, every visit included a stickleback hunt in the big upper pond with the waterfall. They had the knack of being able to retreat under rocks or into the weeds and catching them was more a matter of good fortune than skill. All the same our jam jars were rarely empty, their contents destined for our small fish tank that was also occasionally inhabited by small eels we caught under the Ballyholme River bridge.

The walk along the Glen's network of paths that eventually led to the sea via the lower pond, was occasionally delayed as we searched for wildflowers like the wonderfully named Germander Speedwell, which we'd learn to identify at school. Just reaching the shore at Smelt Mill Bay was like the end of a big adventure.

A free packet with every fourth turn

TAKING care to look both ways when crossing the road, let's visit some of the many family-owned businesses dotted around the Ballyholme area during the 1960s.

The first port of call, at the bottom of our road, was the Waverley Stores, run for decades by Harry Walsh and his family. There could you buy anything from a daily paper to a handful of nails, which would be weighed on the scale and then poured into waxed paper bags, just like they did with the sweets in large glass jars.

Shops on the Groomsport Road, close to the Windmill Road junction.

If pocket money was running low, you didn't even have to go into the shop because an old penny was all you needed to operate the YZ chewing gum machine mounted on the outside wall. You would get a free packet when the arrow on the handle was pointing forward. This very often meant you waited a few minutes in the hope someone else would come along and leave the handle in a 'winning' position.

A narrow lane at the side of Walsh's shop led up to the Donaghadee Road by way of Grove Park. However, for the purposes of this journey the next port of call was Bertie Boston's shop on the Donaghadee Road, just where it joined the Groomsport Road. At the beginning of the Sixties it was known as McCracken's and was run by a couple of elderly women. It was the best place to buy penny bangers at Hallowe'en and no one raised an eyebrow when children as young as six handed over a shilling for a packet of 12 with a couple of spare pennies for a box of matches.

Pausing only to glance in the direction of the town centre to catch sight of the impressive monkey puzzle tree in a garden on the left hand side, the young shopper, with money burning a hole in his pocket, would set off past George Matthews' Corner and up the steep hill to Thornleigh Gardens, passing Maxie McIlwaine's garage along the way. There you could hire a car or buy petrol for five shillings a gallon but someone my age was more likely to hand over a few pennies for a cycle puncture repair kit in a little tin box.

Thornleigh Gardens had quite an array of small businesses, but our route took us directly to Mrs Dunlop's confectionery shop, where they sold the best selection of bubble gum cards. These included *The Man From Uncle* and *Batman* cards in the mid-Sixties, along with the shockingly bloody American Civil War cards from 1967, with each pack of the latter including a reproduction Confederate banknote valued up to $1,000. We probably spent more of our money there than anywhere else as completing sets became an obsession. For every card you needed, there were dozens you didn't need and these were swapped with schoolfriends at breaktime.

It was hard not to dally for a moment at the untidy open ground opposite Thornleigh Gardens that would eventually become Brice Park. Back then, however, known to some by the name Liddy's Dump, it was an adventure playground, with a deep hollow containing a jungle of bushes, a pond and two small hills. Our journey continued along the Donaghadee Road towards Windmill

Road, passing Wrights, another grocery store (just opposite Grovehill Gardens), and behind it, for a time, a market garden. Rankin's Corner Store was at the top of Windmill Road, while our next destination was Dalglish's shop just off Windmill Road. It was one of those long-forgotten family businesses where the sound of the shop bell ringing would summon a member of the Dalglish family from another part of the house. Open all hours, such shops were the lifeblood of any neighbourhood when you realised you'd run out of sugar or eggs late in the evening.

Arriving at the bottom of Windmill Road you were confronted by numerous small businesses on the Groomsport Road. For the Ballyholme youngster nothing could beat Richie McCartney's shop on the corner with Sheridan Drive. He sold newspapers and magazines, sweets and toys and at Hallowe'en offered the best selection of fireworks in the neighbourhood.

A couple of doors from McCartney's was the Sheridan Cake Shop, which advertised each week in the *Spectator* but really didn't need to as the quality of its freshly made cakes and buns was the stuff of legend. Next door was Roy Rosbotham's chemist's shop where I learned an early lesson in fiscal responsibility. They kept a range of cheap but impressive looking cameras, which could take 12 shots on a 120 roll film, and I set my sights on a particular model priced at just 4/6d. My father, however, pointed out that it wasn't the cost of the camera that mattered, but the film and the processing.

Returning along the Groomsport Road, but on the other side of the road, the route towards Waverley

Drive would pass *While Away*, a stationery shop where you could buy strips of coloured paper to make Christmas chains or an Osmeroid fountain pen, the Co-Op store and the R. T. Quinn car showroom. Previously it was W. A. Simpson and Son's garage, a typical car repair business and filling station, which I would occasionally visit with my father when he needed petrol for our Austin A40 car or some paraffin oil for the weed-killing "flame-thrower" my mother used in the garden. We kept the paraffin in a one gallon container my Dad filled from a tap at the back of Simpson's. It was also used to light the coal fire in our front room. Old newspapers, tied into knots and soaked with paraffin, would be set alight and covered with lumps of coal.

The final business along Groomsport Road was Bob Howe's Mace grocery store on the corner of Godfrey Avenue. Bob was a man who knew everything you needed to know, including the secret of the coffee tin. None of his wide-eyed young customers realised, until he told us, that popping open the top of a sealed tin would "let out the wee man." Bob swore blind that if you watched carefully enough you'd see him fly out with the rush of air; even today I still wonder about the "wee man" when I open a new jar of coffee and break the seal. In addition, Bob sold Brook Bond Tea in quarter-pound packets that included free cards covering a large variety of subjects, from British birds and fish to flags and emblems of the world.

His shop was also the only one I knew where you could leave with more money in your pocket that when you arrived. My mother, as well as having her own vegetable patch in the back garden and a line of apple trees, grew an array of fruits, including raspberries, strawberries, loganberries, blackcurrants and gooseberries. Not only did Bob Howe buy my mother's potatoes, he also took a regular supply of gooseberries, which grew in copious quantities in a jungle at the bottom of the garden. Picking them was a pretty thankless task, but Bob was prepared to pay 6d a pound and that would go a long way towards supplementing our pocket money.

If it had been a good crop I'd head back to Mrs Dunlop's in search of that elusive Civil War index card; on a bad day it would just be Walsh's shop and hopes for a lucky fourth turn on the YZ chewing gum machine.

Window to the world

TELEVISION did not dominate our young lives in the way it does in the 21st Century. Most of our playtime was spent out of doors, but the television set did come into its own on wintry afternoons and in the evenings after homework had been completed.

It wasn't until the final months of 1969 that we

BANGOR MEMORY - Enjoying Barry's seafront amusements in August 1961: Hilary Smith and Muriel Simpson (in first car), Lorraine Simpson and Joan Smith (second car), and Carol Savage (third car). *Spectator* picture.

BANGOR MEMORY - Fifth Bangor Cubs who were second in the County Flag competition and winners of the Carswell Shield for the best pack in the town in 1964. Front (from left): Michael McKee, Martin McMullan, Richard Smyth, William Hunter, Gary Dorman. Second row: Richard Hogg, Shane Wolsey, Arnold Parkinson, Geoffrey Bowman, Nicholas Parr, Ian Wilson, Ian Ferguson, David Graham. Third row: Stephen Rowe, Malcolm Rowe, Nigel Boullier, John Thompson, Miss Betty McKee (Akela), Michael Ellison, Michael Arbuckle, David Hitt, Colin Duffy, Jim Overton. Fourth row: Assistant Cub Master Chris Wilson, Patrick Ellison, Assistant Cub Mistress Deirdre Adair, Peter Aicken, Basil O'Fee, Christopher Gaw, Shane Fox, Barry McMullen, Garth McGimpsey, Martin Miller, Assistant Cub Mistress Betty Moorehead and Assistant Cub Mistress Maeve Garrett.
Spectator picture.

acquired our first colour television set, although it would be another year after that before the range of programmes being broadcast in colour justified the expense.

The television that saw our family through the 1960s, a Bush model, had been bought at the turn of the decade following the launch of Ulster Television in 1959. Its predecessor, which could receive only the BBC transmission, had been bought on hire purchase by my parents for the Queen's coronation in 1953. The 10in screen was miniscule by today's standards and was replaced by a superior 14in model that opened up a whole new world of viewing, including the first images from Dallas following President Kennedy's assassination in 1963, England's victory over West Germany in the 1966 World Cup final, and the first men walking on the surface of the Moon in 1969.

The set comprised a wooden box packed with valves and it needed several minutes to literally 'heat up.' It was easy to twist the 'on' knob, dash down to Walsh's shop to buy sweets and be back in time to watch as the screen sprang to life. Switching it off was much simpler; a turn of the knob in the opposite direction produced a bright white dot in the centre of the screen, which quickly disappeared.

There was no such thing as morning or afternoon television, only the boring test card with boring accompanying music. In fact there were only two channels to choose from: Ulster Television and the slightly more staid BBC. The BBC broadcast programmes specifically for little children at lunchtime, under the *Watch With Mother* banner. These included *Picture Book*, *Andy Pandy*, *The Flowerpot Men*, *Tales Of The Riverbank*, *Rag, Tag and Bobtail* and *The Woodentops*. Programmes for slightly older children didn't start until shortly before 5pm.

BANGOR MEMORY - Clandeboye Primary School football team, winners of the cup in the Bangor and District Primary Schools' League in 1967. Back (from left): Mr H. McComb, David Morrow, Jim McAteer, Ronnie Black, William Ervine, Michael Latimer, Mr J. Barrett. Front: David Johnston, Paul Allen, Peter Cooling, Hugh Cruise, Billy McCoubrey, Martin Wolsey and Raymond Claney. *Spectator* picture.

A series of seven dots, representing major towns and cities in Northern Ireland, then appeared on the screen and were joined together, with accompanying chimes. The opening sequence hadn't finished. Presumably it had a name, but as far as viewers were concerned there was a rousing "Dum de dum de dum, rum de dum de dum, diddle de dum dum dum, rum de dum," and so on. It was the same every weekday without fail.

Then the programmes started. Early in the Sixties,

BANGOR MEMORY - Children from St Comgall's Primary School, whose choir and drama group won prizes at a variety of festivals, are pictured in June 1965. Front (from left): Susan McKee, Catherine Thompson, Anne Murray, Margaret Close, Marie McAlorum, Claire McGreevy, Roisin Spruce, Christine Mulvenna, Bridget McCreery, Claire Thompson, Anastasia McInerney, Linda McKee, Bernadette Murray. Second row: Sharon McGrane, Marita Halsall, Barbara Heatley, Anne Curley, Angela Donegan, Jane Mills, Helena Cross, Pauline Connolly, Sharon Gamble, Sandra Dickson, Maria Thompson, Pauline Donohue, Mary Murray, Susan O'Hara. Third row: Maureen McCann, Bernadette Mulligan, Rita Sharvin, Mary Close, Carmel Walsh, Valerie McAteer, Marianne Coyne, Susan Hibbs, Marianne McShane, Sheena McAlinden, Eithne Caproni, Lorena Hughes, Bernice Gilroy. Back: Marianne Bowler, Marianne Barnes, Mimi McAlinden, Maureen McAlister, Dympna Curley, Dympna Caproni, Maureen Allen, Geraldine Callaghan, Eilish Duffy and Angela Jones.
Spectator picture.

between the two channels, favourites included *Blue Peter, Robin Hood, Captain Pugwash* and *Noggin The Nog*, while later in the decade it was *Magpie, The Monkees, Adam Adamant Lives!*, the very new *Star Trek, Do Not Adjust Your Set* and its big brother with attitude, *Monty Python's Flying Circus.*

Then there were the long-running series we'd never miss, like

BANGOR MEMORY - Winners of first prizes at the Bangor Grammar School swimming gala, held at Pickie Pool in September 1968. From left: Garth McGimpsey, Richard O'Fee, Colin Dickenson and Paul Blair.
Spectator picture.

Thunderbirds, *The Man From Uncle*, *The Avengers*, *Danger Man*, *The Prisoner* and a curious, turn-of-the-19th Century British spy drama from 1968 called *Virgin of the Secret Service*, which I insisted on watching each week because my brother detested it.

But nothing came close to *Doctor Who*. Holidays at home and abroad, birthday parties and trips to the cinema were planned around it. The very first episode was broadcast on Saturday 23 November 1963, the day after President Kennedy was assassinated. There was something different about *Doctor Who*. Stories alternated between futuristic encounters with weird and wonderful creatures in far away universes, and what were essentially history lessons with real figures from the past.

By the time I was 10, and long before history had become a serious subject on the school timetable, I'd learned about the Stone Age, Marco Polo, the Aztecs, the French Revolution, Nero and the Romans, King Richard and the Crusades and the Battle of Culloden.

And then there were the Daleks and the Cybermen. I couldn't resist watching them, but both scared the living daylights out me. Not only did they often appear in my dreams, they also haunted me during my waking hours, late into the night. Until the rules were changed with the programme's 21st Century rebirth, the Daleks couldn't climb stairs. They could at 22 Waverley Drive.

Not only that, they'd formed an alliance with the Cybermen and taken up residence in our attic. It was reached by a narrow flight of unlit stairs one had to pass en route to the toilet. I knew a Cyberman, specifically one of those cloth-faced ones from their first episodes, was waiting to grab me. Late night visits to the toilet, even when answering an urgent call of nature, were few and far between and only happened when I was sure the coast was clear of roaming Daleks and I could pass the attic stairway without pausing for breath.

We left that house in 1977, but as far as I'm aware, they might still be there...

The serious bit

I KNOW the exact day, Monday 2 September 1968, when I was first confronted by the reality of our divided society. I started as a First Former at Bangor Grammar School, and although I managed to avoid having my head shoved into a toilet bowl in the annual ritual known as "ducking", I learned for the first time that some people were perceived as being "different."

Arriving home at the end of the first day I blurted out what someone else had told me: "There are two Catholics in my class." Until then I hadn't realised there were different faiths – as far as I was concerned there were people who attended my church at Ballyholme and there were others who went to other churches in the town because they were nearer to where they lived.

Of course, as far as 11-year-olds were concerned, there were definite advantages in being "different," since our two Catholics were permitted to spend the duration of the prayer-based morning assembly sitting in the cloakrooms. "Jammy," we called it.

All the same, with violence beginning to spill onto the streets of Northern Ireland, there was no avoiding the fact that my Ballyholme bubble had been pierced and I was becoming increasingly exposed to the ever-changing outside world.

That same winter Ulster politics came knocking on our front door, as my father Hugh had decided to put his name forward as a prospective candidate for the newly created Bangor seat at Stormont. Quite why was a complete mystery to me. With the benefit of hindsight, I now know that, as a Queen's Counsel, he would have been far from alone at Stormont, which was packed with members of the legal profession.

Certainly my father was ambitious and, having spent much of the Second World War in the RAF, no one would have denied him a tilt at elected office. There was certainly a family history of giving service to the

Official Unionist candidate Bertie Campbell with leading supporters prior to the 1969 Stormont election. Front (from left): Mrs Campbell, D. F. J. McAuley (chairman of the Bangor Unionist Association), Mr Campbell, Fred Tughan. Back: Robert Webb (election agent), Cllr Maisie McMullan (vice-chairman of the Bangor Unionist Association), Dr M. Smyth (chairman of the Clifton Unionists), Alex Beattie, Cllr Jack Preston (chairman of the Dufferin Unionists) and Hugh Bowman QC.
Spectator picture.

community. His grandfather, Alexander Bowman, became the first working class Irishman to stand for Westminster in 1885. Although he was unsuccessful in that endeavour, Alexander served a term from 1897 to 1901 as one of the first Labour members on Belfast Corporation. My grandfather, another Hugh, served as a co-opted member of Bangor Borough Council during the Second World War.

THE COUNTY DOWN SPECTATOR

WHO WILL BE M.P. FOR BANGOR?

Allport walks out of Unionist meeting

Christmas Gifts

Ultimately my father's bid for Stormont failed. He had no political experience and offered his unwavering support as a liberally-minded unionist to Prime Minister Terence O'Neill in his endeavours to bring about change in Northern Ireland. Also, very tellingly, he was not a member of

WARNER'S SHOES

THE COUNTY DOWN SPECTATOR AND ULSTER STANDARD

McCONNELL IS BANGOR'S FIRST M.P.

IN OUR OPINION

Independent beats party machine

NEW M.P.—NEW SEAT

BABINGTON WINS NORTH DOWN: "VICTORY FOR P.M."

CURRIE—I'LL RESIGN IF P.M. STAYS

STEP INTO SPRING

Trend Shop

WHAT'S ON

As smart shoes go these go further.

New Lotus Bucks.

WARNER'S

the Orange Order.

He was runner-up to Bertie Campbell, who had the distinct advantage of being a long-serving member of Bangor Borough Council and Mayor since 1966 and was a prominent local Orangeman. However, Campbell, whose candidature was made unanimous on my father's proposal, lost out at the February 1969 election, following the surprise intervention of blind war veteran Bertie McConnell. The latter stood as an independent unionist, also backing O'Neill, and his majority exceeded 2,500 votes. McConnell's election agent was our next-door neighbour Hubert Nesbitt and it was an early manifestation of what would, in 1970, become the Alliance Party. My mother, who was decidedly more political than my father, would subsequently throw her weight behind Jim Kilfedder in his successful bid to secure the North Down seat in the highly significant Westminster election of June 1970. By then Terence O'Neill and his politics of reconciliation were but a distant memory.

Miss G. Lawrence, "Auntie Gertie" to the girls of Kyle House, snapped after she had snapped Manchester United idol George Best. "Spectator" Photo. 71/14-19.

BEST MOBBED IN BANGOR

My father, his political ambitions now firmly put to bed, took me to see a Northern Ireland side that included George Best play Wales in a Home International match at Windsor Park in May 1969. Six weeks later we travelled to Aldergrove Airport to commence a family holiday, but we took a route that kept us well away from the troublespots that were on the television news each evening. It was obvious, even to a 12-year-old boy, that there was considerable tension in the air.

My Sixties' playground was falling silent. Suddenly it wasn't fun any more.

Dear Reader

I hope you have enjoyed this publication from Ballyhay Books, an imprint of Laurel Cottage Ltd. We publish an eclectic mix of books, ranging from personal memoirs to authoritative books on local history, from sport to poultry, from photographs to fiction and from music to marine interests – but all with a distinctly local flavour.

To see details of these books as well as the beautifully illustrated books of our sister imprint, Cottage Publications, why not visit our website at www.cottage-publications.com or contact us at:–

Laurel Cottage
15 Ballyhay Rd
Donaghadee
Co. Down
N. Ireland
BT21 0NG
Tel: +44 (0)28 9188 8033

Timothy S Johnston

BALLYHAY BOOKS